Simplified Proofreading:
How to Catch Errors Using Fewer Marks

by Peggy Smith

Published by

Editorial Experts, Inc.
66 Canal Center Plaza, Suite 200
Alexandria, VA 22314
703/683-0683

ISBN 0-935012-01X

CONTENTS

INTRODUCTION

What Is Proofreading?

Proofreading involves comparing a new version with an older version of the same material and catching and marking the errors in the new version. For example, proofreaders might compare a handwritten draft with the pages typed from it, or they might compare an author's manuscript with printer's proofs. Sometimes a proofreader reads only the newer version, but this should happen only when the older version is in a form that prevents easy comparison (for example, in shorthand or on tape), or when the older version is lost.

When there are two versions to read, comparison is the key. Reading over the newer version without comparing it to the older one is seldom good enough. The new version might make sense, but important changes and omissions from the old version can go undetected.

Proofreading is done only to material that has already been typed or typeset* from an older version—material that should need no changes except for correction of a few errors. Material that has yet to be entirely typed, retyped, or typeset should be an editor's, not a proofreader's, responsibility.

The important things in proofreading are (1) catching the errors, and (2) marking the errors so the person who must correct them will understand what to do.

Professionally done, proofreading is a skill that requires extensive training, practice, and knowledge of marks and publication processes. If you don't work as a professional proofreader, you may not need such background. However, you may often need to look something over to be sure it is correct. With the

* See *typeset* under "Terms You Need to Know."

techniques in this book, you can quickly learn a lot about what mistakes to look for and how to mark them for correction.

What Is Simplified Proofreading?

Simplified Proofreading is an easy-to-learn modification of the professional proofreading system.

The simplified system is based on techniques that professional proofreaders have used over the centuries. Gone, however, are the intricacies of the professional system and the long list of hieroglyphic-like marks. Only the basic, time-tested, time-saving techniques remain, now available to you in the few hours it will take to read this book and do the exercises.

Who Can Use Simplified Proofreading?

Simplified Proofreading is for you if you are not a typist but must check what has been typed from your draft or your dictation.

It is for you if you are an author who must compare your manuscript to the proofs the publisher typeset from your manuscript (especially if you are the only one who will do this). It is also for you if you are a typist or word processing operator who proofreads your own work, or if you are a typing or word processing supervisor who checks your subordinates' work.

Simplified Proofreading is for any non-professional proofreader who must sometimes read proof.*

Advantages of Simplified Proofreading

Simplified Proofreading has many advantages:

- Most people who need to proofread can learn this system in less than a day.

*If you want to know more about professional proofreading, write to Editorial Experts, Inc., about their book *Mark My Words: Instruction and Practice in Proofreading* (Editorial Experts, Inc., 66 Canal Center Plaza, Suite 200, Alexandria, VA 22314).

- Most people who need to make the corrections a proofreader has marked can learn the Simplified Proofreading marks in a few minutes.

- In an office where several people occasionally proofread, each using different marks, Simplified Proofreading will introduce uniformity, which will make work much easier for the people who make corrections.

- Simplified Proofreading is adaptable to any kind of typing, typesetting, or printing, including word processing and computer output.

- Simplified Proofreading can be used to mark any kind of error.

- The simplified system is compatible with the professional system. Anyone used to professional proofreader's marks will understand Simplified Proofreading marks.

Terms You Need to Know

Key Words

You need to know seven key words:

Copy (as a noun): (1) *The copy* usually means the material that has been prepared for typing or typesetting; that is, a manuscript or draft that will be or has been transferred to a later version. (2) *Copy* is also a general term, as in "handwritten copy," "typed copy," and "typeset copy." (3) And, of course, *a copy* is a reproduction or duplicate of an original work.

A *character* is any single letter of the alphabet, punctuation mark, numeral, or symbol (such as a dollar sign).

Lowercase letters are the small letters of the alphabet; for example:

```
this is a line of lowercase letters

THIS IS A LINE OF CAPITAL (UPPERCASE) LETTERS
```

A *subscript* character goes below the line. For example, the 2 in H_2O is·subscript.

7

A *superscript* character goes above the line. Footnote references are often superscript. The 2 in $3^2 = 9$ is superscript.

Type is a collection of characters put on paper (or other material) mechanically. Typewriters, word processing machines, and typesetting equipment all produce type on a page.

Typeset copy always has many more variables than typewritten copy. A typeset page may have several type sizes and typefaces (see the next paragraph for a description of typefaces). But even a line of typeset copy looks different from a typewritten line. In a typeset line, a W takes more horizontal space than an i, an O takes more space than a period. In a typewritten line, every character takes the same amount of space (except on certain special "proportional spacing" machines). Here are examples of typeset and typewritten lines:

These are typeset lines: ABCDEFGHIJKLMNOP,
abcdefghijklmnop.

These are typewritten lines: ABCDEFGHIJKLMNOPQRSTUVWXYZ,
abcdefghijklmnopqrstuvwxyz.

Typefaces

You need to know three terms for typefaces:

Roman type is standard, upright type. You normally see it in books and newspapers:

This is a line typeset in roman type

Italic type is sloped. It is used for emphasis and in many titles:

This is a line typeset in italic type

This is a line typed in italic type

Boldface type is heavier type with thicker lines. Boldface can be either italic or roman:

This is a line typeset in boldface roman

This is a line typeset in boldface italic

Abbreviations

You need to know four abbreviations:

cap(s): capital letter(s)

lc: lowercase

caps + *lc*: capitals and lowercase, for example:

```
This is a Line Typed in Capitals and Lowercase
```

This is a Line Typeset in Capitals and Lowercase

sp: instruction to spell out the abbreviation, numeral, or symbol

GENERAL RULES

To do Simplified Proofreading, you must follow five general rules:

Rule 1. Mark Only on Material You Will Not Harm

For Simplified Proofreading, you need to make proofreading marks directly on the latest version of the material. However, do not mark an original that cannot be replaced. Mark only carbon copies, printer's proofs (called *galleys* and *page proofs*), photocopies, other machine copies, printouts (such as from a word processor), or hard copy (such as from a computerized machine).

If you have only the original of something—a letter, address labels, or camera-ready copy (pages ready to be photographed and printed)—get a copy made before you mark. Working only with originals usually requires special equipment or techniques.*

Rule 2. Write Clearly and Mark Neatly

Simplified Proofreading fails if your handwriting or your marks will be misread. If anyone has ever complained that your handwriting is hard to read, you must print.

For printing, use the following alphabet:

Block capitals:

ABCDEFGHIJKLMNOP
QRSTUVWXYZ

---

* One of the special techniques is writing out a list of errors, including the page, paragraph, and line number for each error. A sample list, using this tedious technique, appears in Appendix A.

Lowercase:**

$$a\ b\ c\ d\ e\ f\ g\ h\ i\ j\ k\ l\ (or\ \ell)\ m\ n\ o\ p$$
$$q\ r\ (or\ \text{\textit{r}})\ s\ t\ u\ v\ w\ x\ y\ z$$

If your cursive or "script" handwriting is good, use it. But whether you write or print, space your characters so that no one can mistake one word for two or two words for one, and be sure to make capitals distinctly larger than lowercase letters.

Rule 3. Make Marks in Pairs

Always make two marks for every correction, one right in the line of type (the text) and one in the margin.

The mark in the text pinpoints where a correction is needed. The mark in the margin tells what to do at the point marked in the text. For example, to add a missing *r*, make the two marks shown:

poofreading

There are good reasons for marking in pairs:

- It is hard for the person making the corrections to search an entire page for tiny in-text marks and changes; they are easy to overlook. The mark in the margin shows at a glance that there is a problem and the mark in the text pinpoints the problem.

- Most material to be proofread does not have enough room for writing between the lines (as an editor would on double-spaced typewritten pages).

- Marking in pairs is the traditional system; most professional proofreaders and typesetters understand it.

**When *l* and *r* stand alone, avoid using the printed forms *l* and *r* ; use the written forms ℓ and ⟂ .

11

Rule 4. Make Marginal Marks from Left to Right and Use Slashes to Separate Marks

If two or more different corrections must be made in the same line, write the marginal marks from left to right. Use slashes to separate the marks. For example, to add a missing *r* and a missing *d*, mark as shown:

r/d   poofreaing

If the same correction must be made more than once consecutively in the same line, repeat the mark. For example, to add an *r* three times, do the following:

r/r/r   poofeading maks

Use both margins. Choose the margin closer to the error; for example:

i / t /m   Thry days hath Septeber, April, June an Noember.   d/v

You need not be precise about dividing the page down the middle to make marks at the left and right. Just make it a general rule to use both margins as best you can.

Once you get used to it, you will find using both margins practical for these reasons:

● You get more room; two margins are better than one.

● You make less of an effort. If you marked only in the right margin, for example, and found an error on the far left of the page, after marking the text you would have to move your eye and your pencil all the way across the page to make the mark in the margin.

Rule 5. Draw a Ring Around Marginal Marks When You Are Giving Instructions Not to Be Typed or Typeset

A ring around a mark in the margin means "Follow these instructions but don't type or typeset letters that appear in the ring."

The ring is very useful. You can tell the person making the corrections exactly what to do; for example:

Text With Error	Proofreader's Marks in Text	Proofreader's Marks in Margin	Corrected Copy
S75	$75	$ (dollar sign)	$75
20,000	20,000	0 (zero)	20,000
No. 3	No. 3	# (number sign)	#3
one %	one %	1 (figure)	1%

FIVE CLASSES OF CORRECTION

There are five classes of correction:

1. Taking out type

2. Adding type

3. Replacing wrong characters with right ones

4. Changing typeface or type style

5. Changing the spacing or position of type.

Each class of correction has its own special kind of proofreading mark. If you master the special marks, you will make things easier for yourself and for the person who must interpret your marks.

Taking Out Type

How to Mark

Marking to take out type is simple. First, mark through the type you don't want. Next, write the take-out (delete) sign (ℱ) in the margin. Here is an example:

ℱ   Proofreadingȿ

The best way to mark out something in the text depends on how long the take-out is.

One or Two Characters

To take out one or two characters, first slash through each of them in the text. Do not black them out; the person making the correction must be able to read the characters. Next write the take-out sign ( ) in the margin. For example, to take out an extra *g*, mark as shown:

proofreading*g̸*

To take out two side-by-side characters, mark as shown:

*p̸f̸*proofreading

More than Two Characters

To take out more than two characters, a whole word, or an entire line, first mark a line through everything that must go. Be careful to mark out neither more nor less than you mean to. Be sure that what you mark out can still be read. Next make a take-out sign in the margin; for example:

~~proof~~proofreading

Several Lines

To take out several entire, consecutive lines, mark each line out and write one large take-out sign; for example:

```
Now is the time
for all good men
for all good men
for all good men
and women to come
to the aid of
their country.
```

A Long Passage

To take out a long passage or a whole page, draw a box around it, mark a big X through it, and write a large take-out sign in the margin; for example:

To take out a long passage or a whole page, draw a box around it, mark a big X through it, and write the take-out sign in the margin, for example:

Simplified Proofreading

Repeated Characters

If you need to take out characters, words, or lines that are repeated by mistake, you have to decide which set to mark.

You should mark repetitions at the beginnings and ends of words to leave the words whole, like this:

~~proof~~proofreading

proofreading~~ing~~

It seldom matters which repetition you mark out in the middle of a word or sentence (or which entire line you mark out). Here, for example, either choice would be correct:

proo/freading

proof/reading

proofreading is ~~quality~~ quality control

proofreading is quality ~~quality~~ control

New Spacing

Ordinarily, you should not try to mark for the new spacing that may be needed when characters are taken out. Leave these spacing changes to the typist or typesetter.

A Good Way to Work the Exercises

On the next page are the first of the practice exercises this book provides to help you remember what you have read.

The best way to learn is by doing *while you tell yourself what you are doing*. Talk to yourself as you work every exercise. For example, while you work the first line of Practice 2, say "To take out the extra 3, I slash through it; then I mark the take-out sign in the margin." While you work the next line, you might shorten the conversation to "Slash, take out. Slash, take out. Slash, take out."

This is an excellent technique for self-study. Try it!

In practice 2 and other practice exercises, mark on both sides of the righthand column; for example:

Lefthand
Column

Righthand
Column

Simplified Proofreading   ℐ   Simplif/ied Proofreading ~~Reading~~   ℐ

When you have finished every exercise, compare your marks one by one to the answer key in Appendix E. Analyze the kinds of errors you missed, notice what marks you are making wrong, and invent your own corrective exercises.

PRACTICE 1. THE TAKE-OUT SIGN

Practice making the take-out sign until it is as easy as writing your own name:

Connect the dots:

Now make small take-out signs ($\mathcal{S}$) to fill the rest of the page.

PRACTICE 2. TAKING OUT TYPE

Compare the column on the left below to the column on the right. Mark the righthand column so that, when corrections are made, it will match the lefthand column exactly.

1234567890	12334567890
abcdefghijklmnopqrstuvwxyz	abxcdefghijkylmnopqrstzuvwxyz
1970	1970
1971	19710
1972	1972
1973	1973
1974	1969
1975	1974
1976	1975
1977	1976
1978	1977
1979	1978
	231979

```
Thirty days hath September,        Thirtyt days hath September,
April, June, and November.         April, May, June, and November.
All the rest have thirty-one       All the rest have thirty-oney
Save February, which alone         Save Feb February, which alone
Has twenty-eight,                  Has twenty-eight,
   and one day more                   and one day more
Is added to each year in four.     Is added to each years in four.


Life is our dictionary. . . .      Life is your dictionary. . . .
Life lies behind us as the         Life lies right behind us as the
quarry from whence we get          quarry from whence we get
tiles and copestones for the       tiles and copestones for the
masonry of today.  This is         masonary of today.  This is
the way to learn grammar.          the way to learn grammar.
Colleges and books only copy       Colleges and books only just copy
the language which the field       the language which the field
and the work-yard made.            and also the work-yard made.
          Ralph Waldo Emerson              by Ralph Waldo Emerson
          The American Scholar             in The American Scholar
```

Adding Type

How to Mark

Marking to add type is simple. First make a pointer (arrowhead or caret) like this: **∧** in the text, pointing up to the place in the line where the addition belongs. Next write in the margin what the addition is. Whether or not you write out the whole addition in the margin depends on how long the addition is.

Short Additions

To add just a few characters or words, first make a pointer (**∧**) in the text where the addition belongs. Next write the entire addition in the margin; for example:

ɾ‌ʅ   p⌄oofreading

You need only one pointer for as many characters or words as are needed in one spot (up to five or six words); for example:

is the first step   proofreading⌄toward quality control

Long Additions

There often is not enough room in the margin to write out more than six words. Besides, you can make a mistake or get sloppy in writing so much. So, instead of writing long additions, after you place a pointer where you want to add to the line, tell the person making corrections where to find the addition in the old comparison copy. Write the page number of the old copy in the margin and circle the instruction: ⟨add from p. ___⟩ (fill in the number). Make sure you attach the old copy to the new so the typist or typesetter can find the addition.

If you are not comparing the copy you are reading to an older version, and if you know what needs to be added, write the long addition on a separate piece of paper. In the margin of the page you are proofreading, write ⟨add attached⟩ Then attach the written-out addition with a paperclip or masking tape. If there is more than one long addition on a page, label each one according to an "ABC" key: (⟨add A attached⟩ , ⟨add B attached⟩ .)

Use of Slashes

When more than one pointer is needed in the same line, use slashes to separate your marks in the margin; for example:

r/r   poofreading this lie

If you think it is necessary, lengthen one line of the pointer to show exactly where an addition goes; for example:

r   poofreading

Sometimes you may need a sideways pointer to mark between lines, for example:

```
              100
3oo        > 200
              400
              500
```

If you think it is necessary to show exactly where an addition goes, you can lengthen one line of the sideways pointer, like this:

```
              100
300      >   200
              400
              500
```

New Spacing

Ordinarily, you should not try to mark for the new spacing that may be needed when characters are added. Leave these spacing changes to the typist or typesetter.

PRACTICE 3. ADDING TYPE

Compare the column on the left below to the column on the right. Mark the righthand column so that, when corrections are made, it will match the lefthand column exactly. Compare your marks to the answer key in Appendix E.

1234567890

abcdefghijklmnopqrstuvwxyz

1970
1971
1972
1973
1974
1975
1976
1977
1978
1979

123567890

acdefghijlmnopqrsuvwxyz

1970
1971

1973
1974
1975
196
1977
1978

979

```
Thirty days hath September,
April, June, and November.
All the rest have thirty-one
Save February, which alone
Has twenty-eight,
   and one day more
Is added to each year in four.

Life is our dictionary. . . .
Life lies behind us as the
quarry from whence we get
tiles and copestones for the
masonry of today.  This is
the way to learn grammar.
Colleges and books only copy
the language which the field
and the work-yard made.
          Ralph Waldo Emerson
          The American Scholar
```

```
Thirty days hath September,
Aril, June, November.
All the rest have thirty-ne
Save, which alone
Has twent-eght,
   and one day more
Is added to each yer in four.

Life is our ditionary. . . .
Life lies behind as the
quarry fro whence we get
tiles and copstones for the
masony of today.  This is
the way to learn.
Coleges and books copy
the language the field
and the work-yar made.
          Emerson
          The American Scholar
```

PRACTICE 4. TAKING OUT AND ADDING TYPE

Compare the column on the left below to the column on the right. Mark the righthand column for adding and taking out so that, when corrections are made, it will match the lefthand column exactly. Compare your marks to the answer key in Appendix E.

We all know that as the	We know that just as the
human body can be nourished	humane body cannot be nourished
on any food, though it were	on any food, although
boiled grass and the broth	boiled grass and the broth
of shoes, so the human mind	of old shoes, so the human mind
can be fed by any knowledge.	can be fed by fled by any knowledge.
And great and heroic men	And many great and heroical men
have existed who had almost	have had almost
no other information than by	no other informations than by
the printed page. I would	printed pages. I would
only say that it needs a	only say that surely it needs a
strong head to bear that diet.	very strong head that diet.

Replacing Wrong Characters with Right Ones

How to Mark

To replace (substitute for) wrong characters with right ones, first mark out the wrong characters in the text. Next write the correct characters in the margin. For example, to replace an *l* with a *d*, mark as shown:

d   proofrea̸ding

To replace two characters that are side by side, mark out each one separately as shown:

ro   pr̸o̸ofreading

To replace three or more characters that are next to each other, mark horizontally as shown:

hath   Thirty days ~~for~~ September

These are the same in-text marks you use to take out characters. The big difference is the mark in the margin. To take characters out, make a take-out sign in the margin. To replace wrong characters, write the correct characters in the margin.

One mark in the text takes care of as many or as few characters or words as are needed in that spot. For example, a single letter can be replaced by several letters. The following line shows how to mark "sing" to replace it with "proofreading":

proofread   s̸ing

The last part of a word, plus the word next to it, can be replaced by letters that change the word's ending. The following example shows how to mark "proofreader's marks" to replace it with "proofreading":

ing   proofread~~er's marks~~

Several words can be replaced by one word, or one word can be replaced by several; for example:

hath   Thirty days ~~are all there are in~~ September,

All the rest ~~Others~~ have thirty-one.

Uses of Replacement

Replacement is a useful technique. If you can't quickly figure out what's wrong with a word, mark through the entire word and write it correctly in the margin, for example:

proofreading ~~phooferaeding~~

Marking to replace a whole word is almost always the easiest way to fix a word that needs more than one kind of correction, as in the last example.

Sometimes replacement of an entire word is not only the easiest but the best way; for example, to change "forbid" to "permit":

Best: ~~forbid~~   *permit*

Too complicated: *f̷o̷r̷b̷i̷d̷*   *p/e/m/t*

Always try to mark in the clearest and most efficient way.

PRACTICE 5. REPLACING WRONG CHARACTERS WITH RIGHT ONES

Compare the column on the left below to the column on the right. Mark the righthand column so that, when corrections are made, it will match the lefthand column exactly. Compare your marks to the answer key in Appendix E.

1234567890	1264567890
abcdefghijklmnopqrstuvwxyz	abxdefghijkymnopqrszuvwxyz
1970	1970
1971	1970
1972	1972
1973	1973
1974	1974
1975	1975
1976	1942
1977	1977
1978	1978
1979	2001

Thirty days hath September,	Thirty days hath July,
April, June, and November.	April, Jane, and November.
All the rest have thirty-one	All the rest number thirty-one
Save February, which alone	Save Saturday, which alone
Has twenty-eight,	Has twunty-eight,
and one day more	and one day more
Is added to each year in four.	Is added to every one in four.

Life is our dictionary. . . .	Life is our encyclopedia. . . .
Life lies behind us as the	Life lies ahead of us as the
quarry from whence we get	quarry from whence we acquire
tiles and copestones for the	tiles and copestones for the
masonry of today. This is	bricklaying of today. This is
the way to learn grammar.	how we learn grammar.
Colleges and books only copy	Colleges and schools only copy
the language which the field	the language which the laborers
and the work-yard made.	in the work-yard made.
Ralph Waldo Emerson	Ralph Frodo Emerson
The American Scholar	The American Scholar

Transposing

Some people use a double loop to mark transposed (exchanged) characters or words. If this is easy for you, do it. First, mark a double loop (∿) around the characters that should be exchanged with each other. Next write ⟨tr⟩ (for transpose) in the margin; for example:

Transposition, however, is just another kind of replacement. It's often just as easy to mark this kind of problem as a replacement, like this:

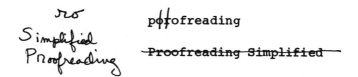

Do not mark characters or words for transposing unless they are right next to each other.

It is a poor idea to transpose numbers; they're too easily mixed up. Always *replace* numbers; for example:

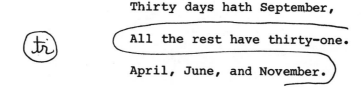

You can transpose lines or paragraphs with a horizontal double loop; for instance:

    Thirty days hath September,

⟨tr⟩   All the rest have thirty-one.

    April, June, and November.

Another way to switch lines is to mark one line to be moved to where it belongs. In this case, "tr" means "transfer."

```
Thirty days hath September,

All the rest have thirty-one.                    tr

April, June, and November.
```

PRACTICE 6 (OPTIONAL). TRANSPOSING

Do this exercise if you want to practice using the special marks for transposing. Compare the column on the left to the column on the right. Mark corrections in the righthand column with the double loop in the text and ⟨tr⟩ in the margin. Compare your marks to those in the answer key in Appendix E.

1.	Mark "houseboat" to make "boathouse."	houseboat
2.	Mark "racehorse" to make "horserace."	racehorse
3.	Mark "songbird" to make "birdsong."	songbird
4.	Mark "silver coin" to make "coin silver."	silver coin
5.	Mark "human being" to make "being human."	human being
6.	Mark "How is she wrong?" to make "How wrong is she?"	How is she wrong?
7.	Mark "lien" to make "line."	lien
8.	Mark "trail" to make "trial."	trail
9.	Mark "silver" to make "sliver."	silver
10.	Mark "barn" to make "bran."	barn
11.	Mark "casual" to make "causal."	casual
12.	Mark "stake" to make "takes."	stake
13.	Mark "sword" to make "words."	sword
14.	Mark "procede" to make "proceed."	procede
15.	Mark "bear" to make "bare."	bear
16.	Mark "grate" to make "great."	grate
17.	Mark "ware" to make "wear."	ware
18.	Mark "seat" to make "sate."	seat
19.	Mark "bake" to make "beak."	bake
20.	Mark "aide" to make "idea."	aide
21.	Mark "range" to make "anger."	range

PRACTICE 7. TAKING OUT, ADDING, AND REPLACING TYPE

Compare the column on the left below to the column on the right. Mark the righthand column so that, when corrections are made, it will match the lefthand column exactly. Compare your marks to the answer key in Appendix E.

Over the office door of Aldus	Above the office door or Aldius
Manutius (1450-1515), founder	Manutius (1540-1515), founder
of the Aldine Press in Venice,	of the Alden Press in Nence,
appeared this legend: Whoever	appeared this motto: Whoever
you are, you are earnestly re-	you may be, you are earnesly re-
quested by Aldus to state your	quested by Aldus to state your
business briefly and to take	bisiness briefly and to take
your departure promptly. In	your leave promptily. In
this way you may be of service	this manner you may service
even as was Hercules to the	even as did Hercules
weary Atlas, for this is a	for this is a
place of work for everyone who	place of worship for everyoen who
enters.	enter.

Changing Typeface or Type Style

How to Mark

When the characters in the text are the right ones, but the typeface or the style of type is wrong, carefully draw a ring around the characters in the text. Then, in another ring in the margin, write out the instructions.

The ring in the text means something a little different from the ring in the margin. In the text, the ring means, "These are the characters the instruction in the margin tells you about." In the margin, the ring means, "This is an instruction. Do not put the characters you are reading into type."

To replace a capital letter with lowercase, mark as shown:

 pRoofreading

To replace a lowercase letter with a capital, mark as shown:

 Jane jones

Every ring in the text needs a separate mark in the margin. For example, to replace two words in "all caps" style with "caps and lowercase" style, mark as shown:

	Proofreader's Mark	*Correction Done*
	SIMPLIFIED PROOFREADING	Simplified Proofreading

You can ring an entire word or phrase and mark it "all caps," even though some of the characters are already capitalized, like this:

	Proofreader's Mark	*Correction Done*
	John Smith	JOHN SMITH

You can also ring an entire group of characters and mark it "all lc;" for example:

	Proofreader's *Mark*	*Correction* *Done*
all *lc*	Proofreading: The First Step to Quality Control	Proofreading: the first step to quality control

Here are some examples of how to mark to replace the wrong style of type. In every case, the wrong type style has a ring around it and instructions for the right style are in a ring in the margin.

Correction Needed	Proofreader's Marks		Correction Done
replace a lowercase letter with a capital	*(Cap)*	ⓟroofreading	Proofreading
replace a capital with a lowercase letter	*(lc)*	Ⓟroofreading	proofreading
replace all lowercase letters with capitals	*(Caps)*	(proofreading)	PROOFREADING
replace all capital letters with lowercase	*(lc)*	(PROOFREADING)	proofreading
replace all caps style with caps and lowercase style	*(lc)*	ⓅROOFREADING	Proofreading
replace all lowercase style with caps and lowercase style	*(cap)*	ⓟroofreading	Proofreading
replace roman type with italic	*(italic)*	(proofreading)	*proofreading*
replace italic type with roman	*(roman)*	*(proofreading)*	proofreading
replace regular type with boldface	*(boldface)*	(proofreading)	**proofreading**
replace regular italic type with boldface italic	*(boldface italic)*	*(proofreading)*	***proofreading***
replace roman all caps style with italic caps and lowercase style	*(italic Caps + lc)*	(PROOFREADING)	*Proofreading*
replace caps and lowercase style with all caps	*(all caps)*	(Proofreading)	PROOFREADING
replace boldface type with regular type	*(regular, not boldface)*	**PROOFREADING**	PROOFREADING

33

PRACTICE 8. CHANGING TYPEFACE AND TYPE STYLE

Review the sections on typefaces and abbreviations at the beginning of the book. Compare the column on the left below to the column on the right. Mark the righthand column so that, when corrections are made, it will match the lefthand column exactly. Compare your marks to the answer key in Appendix E.

WORDS ABOUT WORDS	**Words About Words**
Epigrams	*Epigrams*
A powerful agent is the right word. —*Mark Twain*	A powerful agent is the right word. —Mark Twain
Longer than deeds liveth the word. —*Pindar*	*Longer than deeds liveth the word.* —*PINDAR*
Be not the slave of words. —*Carlyle*	Be not the slave of words. —*Carlyle*
Words are stubborn things. —*Zartman*	*Words are stubborn things.* —Zartman
Words make love. —*Andre Breton*	**WORDS MAKE LOVE.** **—Andre Breton**
A word, once sent abroad, flies irrevocably. —*Horace*	A Word, Once Sent Abroad, Flies Irrevocably. —*Horace*
People who say they love words are the biggest bores of all. —*Minor*	People who say they love words are the biggest bores of all. —*Minor*
Words pay no debts. —*Shakespeare*	Words pay no debts. **—Shakespeare**
Syllables govern the world. —*John Selden*	Syllables govern the world. —*John Selden*

Punctuation and Symbols

Professional proofreaders use special marks for punctuation marks and for many symbols. You do not have to know these special marks. All you have to do is mark in the text for adding or replacing; then, in the margin, write out the name of the punctuation mark or symbol and draw a ring around the name, for example:

	Proofreader's Mark	*Corrected Copy*
(apostrophe)	a proofreaders mark	a proofreader's mark
(comma)	red white, and blue	red, white, and blue
(subscript 2)	H₂O	H_2O

You must write out the words "comma" or "apostrophe" unless there is no possible way a handwritten **,** in the margin could be misinterpreted. It is safe to write **,** only if the comma or apostrophe you want is part of a group of characters you must write in the margin for addition or replacement; for example:

	Proofreader's Mark	*Corrected Copy*
er's	a proofread mark	a proofreader's mark
Red,	white, and blue	Red, white, and blue

(The professional proofreaders' marks for punctuation and symbols are listed in Appendix B. If you use these marks, be very sure that the person making the corrections knows them. The marks' meanings are not obvious and the marks take a little getting used to.)

Review

Summary of Four Classes of Marks

To take out type:

- *in the text*, mark out the characters

  — slash one or two characters (/)

  — make a line through three or more characters, a word, a line of type, or several lines of type

- *in the margin*

  — make the take-out sign (ℐ).

To add type:

- *in the text*, make a pointer

  — in a line of type, make a pointer pointing up (Λ)

  — between lines, make a pointer pointing sideways (>)

- *in the margin*

  — for short additions (up to five or six words)—

    • write the letters to be added

    • write out and put a ring around the name of the punctuation marks to be added

  — for long additions (more than five or six words), tell where to find the addition by—

- writing ⬭ add from p. ___ ⬭ , giving the page number in the old copy, or

- writing out the addition on a separate piece of paper, giving it an alphabetical key, and writing in the margin; for example, (add B attached)

To replace wrong characters with right ones:

- *in the text*, mark out the wrong characters

  — slash one or two characters (/)

  — make a line through three or more characters

- *in the margin*

  — write the correct letters

  — write out and put a ring around the name of the correct punctuation mark.

To replace the wrong type style:

- *in the text*

  — put a ring around the characters to be changed

- *in the margin*

  — write the instructions inside a ring.

PRACTICE 9. REVIEW OF MARKS

Do the following exercises, marking as efficiently as possible.
Compare your marks to the answer key in Appendix E.

1.	Take away from "now" to make "no."	now
2.	Take away from "there" to make "here."	there
3.	Take away from "pencil" to make "pen."	pencil
4.	Take away from "grandchild" to make "child."	grandchild
5.	Take away from "friend" to make "fiend."	friend
6.	Take away from "exist" to make "exit."	exist
7.	Take away from "display" to make "play."	display
8.	Take away from "proofread" to make "read."	proofread
9.	Take away from "bellow" to make "below."	bellow
10.	Take away from "language" to make "age."	language
11.	Take away from "complete" to make "compete."	complete
12.	Take away from "whole" to make "hole."	whole
13.	Add to "no" to make "now."	no
14.	Add to "here" to make "there."	here
15.	Add to "pen" to make "pencil."	pen
16.	Add to "child" to make "grandchild."	child
17.	Add to "fiend" to make "friend."	fiend
18.	Add to "exit" to make "exist."	exit
19.	Add to "play" to make "display."	play
20.	Add to "read" to make "proofread."	read
21.	Add to "below" to make "bellow."	below

22.	Add to "age" to make "language."	age
23.	Add to "compete" to make "complete."	compete
24	Add to "hole" to make "whole."	hole
25.	Replace "sensible" with "sensibly."	sensible
26.	Replace "unto" with "into."	unto
27.	Replace "type" with "typical."	type
28.	Replace "borrow" with "tomorrow."	borrow
29.	Replace "use" with "usage."	use
30.	Replace "survey" with "surveillance."	survey
31.	Replace "scholar" with "scholastic."	scholar
32.	Replace "father" with "mother."	father
33.	Replace "near" with "far."	near
34.	Replace "exercise" with "exorcise."	exercise
35.	Replace "flour" with "flower."	flour
36.	Replace "deported" with "reported."	deported

PRACTICE 10. PROOFREADING REVIEW EXERCISE

Compare the lefthand column below to the column on the right. Mark the righthand column so that, when corrections are made, it will match the lefthand column exactly. Compare your marks to the answer key in Appendix E.

WHICH CAME FIRST?	Which Came First?
Were there no readers, there	Were ther no readers, there
certainly would be no writers;	would not be writers;
clearly therefore, the existence	clearling therefore, the existance
of writers depends upon the	of writers dependent upon the
existence of readers and, of	existents of readers and,
course, since the cause must	yet, because the case must
be antecedent to the effect,	be antecedent to the cause,
readers existed before writers.	all readers existed before writers.
Yet, on the other hand, if there	Yet, on the other hand, If there
were no writers there could be	was no writer there could be
no readers, so it would appear	no readers, so it appears
that writers must be antecedent	that writers must be anticedent
to readers.	to readers.
--Horace Smith, quoted in	--Smitn, quted in
<u>The Love Affairs of a</u>	<u>The Love Affair of a</u>
<u>Bibliomaniac</u> by Eugene Field	<u>Biblomaniac</u> by Eugene Field

CHANGING THE SPACING OR POSITIONING OF TYPE

Six Kinds of Correction

There are six kinds of correction for space and position. You may need to tell the corrector to do any of the following:

- Add space

- Take out some extra space

- Take out all extra space

- Correct the paragraphing

- Align type

- Move characters or blocks of type.

Three Special Marks

Three special marks help solve spacing problems:

The space mark: #

  means "space"

The close-up mark: ◡

  means "close-up or bump (move characters together); leave no extra space"

The paragraph sign: ¶

  means "start a new paragraph here."

41

The Space Mark: How to Add Space

The symbol # stands for "space." Use it any time you want to give instructions that would use the word "space."

To *add* blank space between words or between lines, use the same mark in text you use to add type. Mark an upright pointer between words or a sideways pointer between lines. In the margin, mark "#." Here are examples:

```
Now is the time                              #
for all good men
and all good women                      ⟍ #
to come to the aid
of their country.
```

In proofreading, the only thing "#" means is "space." When *marking*, do not use this symbol to mean anything else. But if you need the symbol typed or typeset, you can make that clear; for example:

	Proofreader's Mark	Correction Done
# (number sign)	#1, #2, ∧3, #4, #5	#1, #2, #3, #4, #5

The Close-Up Mark: How to Take Out Space

How you mark to take out space depends on how much space you want to take out. To take out *all* extra space, mark both in the text and the margin with the close-up sign (◠)—which means "move characters together; leave no extra space," for example:

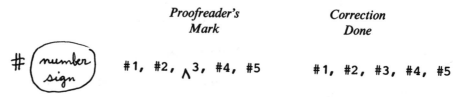

```
⌒      Thirty days hath September,
⌒      April, June, and November⌒.
```

To take out *some* but not *all* extra space, mark only one curved line in the text (half a close-up mark) and the instruction in the margin; for example:

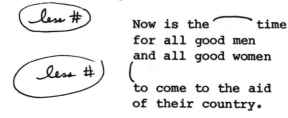

```
(less #)      Now is the ⌒ time
              for all good men
              and all good women
(less #)      (
              to come to the aid
              of their country.
```

The Paragraph Mark

The symbol **⁋** stands for "paragraph." Use it to show where a paragraph begins, for example:

Marked Copy

⁋

Xxxxxxxxxxxxxxxxxxxxxx
xxxxxxxxxxx. Yxxxxxxxxxxxxx
xxxxxxxxxxxxxxxxxxxxxxxxxxxx
xxxxxxxx. ∧Zxxxxxxxxxxxxxxxx
xxxxxxxxxxxxxxxxxxxxxxxxx.

Corrected Copy

Xxxxxxxxxxxxxxxxxxxxxx
xxxxxxxxxxx. Yxxxxxxxxxxxxx
xxxxxxxxxxxxxxxxxxxxxxxxxxxx
xxxxxxx.
   Zxxxxxxxxxxxxxxxxxxxxx
xxxxxxxxxxxxxxxxx.

Use "no **⁋**" to show when a paragraph does not begin; for example:

Marked Copy

(no **⁋**)

Axxxxxxxxxxxxxxxxxxxxxx
xxxxxxxxxxxx. Bxxxxxxxxxxxx
xxxxxxxx.
   ∧Cxxxxxxxxxxxxxxxxxxxx
xxxxxxxxxxxx.

Corrected Copy

Axxxxxxxxxxxxxxxxxxxxxx
xxxxxxxxxxxx. Bxxxxxxxxxxxx
xxxxxxxx. Cxxxxxxxxxxxxxx
xxxxxxxxxxxxxxxxx.

How to Mark Alignment Problems

When type does not line up as it should up and down the page (vertically), mark where the type belongs and write (align) and the additional instructions if necessary; for example:

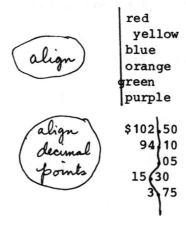

align

|red
  yellow
|blue
|orange
green
|purple

align decimal points

$102|50
  94|10
    |05
  15|30
   3|75

When type does not line up as it should across the page (horizontally), make a line over and under the type in the text and write (align) in the margin. Use this mark for a crooked line, for words out of line, or for one or more badly aligned characters; for example:

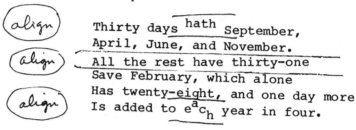

(align)   Thirty days <u>hath</u> September,
         April, June, and November.
(align)   All the rest have thirty-one
         Save February, which alone
         Has twenty-eight, and one day more
(align)   Is added to each year in four.

How to Mark to Move Type

To move type, draw lines to show what you want done and then explain. Three sides of a box work like a magnet, to push or pull type to the place it belongs; for example:

(more left)   One   Six
              Two   Seven
              Three   Eight   *(more right)*
              Four   Nine
              Five   Ten

You can also use "magnets" to mark type to move up or move down:

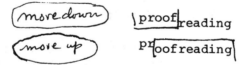

(move down)   \proof|reading

(move up)   pr|oofreading|

To center a line, such as a headline, mark magnets on both sides and write (center) in the margin, as shown:

Marked Copy   *Corrected Copy*

(Center)   ]HEADLINE[HEADLINE

Sometimes a problem can be marked in more than one way. For example, (move left) can sometimes be marked (align). The important thing is not how you mark but that you see the problem and mark it so the corrector knows what you want.

To move a whole block of type to another place on the page, box the block of type and use an arrow to show where you want it moved. Mark it "tr" for "transfer"; for example:

```
         Xxxxxxxxxxxxxxxxxxx
         xxxxxxxxxxxxxxxxxxxxxx
         xxxxxxxxxxx.
            Xxxxxxxxxxxxxxxxxx
         xxxxxxxxxxxxxxxxxxxxxxx
         xxxxxxxxxxx.                    (tr)
            Xxxxxxxxxxxxxxxxxx
         xxxxxxxxxxxxxxxxxxxxxx
         xxxxxxxxxxx.
            Xxxxxxxxxxxxxxxxxx
         xxxxxxxxx.
```

To move a block of type to another page, first, put a box around the block and mark it (move to p.), filling in the new page number. Then, on the page where the type goes, put a pointer in the text and, in the margin, write (add from p.), filling in the old page number.

When characters or words go on the next line, mark as shown:

```
Thirty days hath September, |April,        ( move to
June, and November.                          next line )
```

When a new line is begun by mistake, mark as shown:

```
( one      Now is the time for all
  line )   good men and all good women to come to the aid of their country.
```

When characters or words should be moved back to the line above, mark as shown:

```
( move to        Thirty days hath
  line above )    September, )April, June, and November.
```

Rulers

You will find rulers for typewritten copy in Appendix C, and a ruler for typeset copy in Appendix D. These rulers will help you check to see if typists or typesetters have used the specified measurements for line width, page depth, margin width, and type size.

PRACTICE 11. SPACING MARKS

This exercise is not one in which you compare two versions. Spacing errors are usually errors you need to find only in the new version. In the copy below, find at least one case of each of the following errors and mark the errors. (The errors are not listed below in the order they appear in the exercise.)

add space between lines

make less space between lines

add space between characters

close up space between characters

make less space between characters

align characters

move characters down

move characters up

put on one line

Compare your marks to the answer key in Appendix E.

NEW VERSION ONLY

John Stuart Mill's inaugural address (as rector of the University of St. Andrew) on February 1, 1867, included the following words: "To question all things;--never to turn away from any difficulty, to accept no doctrine either from ourselves or from other people without a rigid scrutiny by negative criticism; letting no fallacy, or incoherence, or confusion of thought, step by unperceived; above

all, to insist upon having the meaning of aword clearly understood before using it, and the meaning of a proposition be fore assenting to it;--these
are the lessons we learn from ancient   dialecticians."

REVIEW

Marks in the Text	*Meaning*
pointer (∧)	add characters or space here, as marked in the margin
marked-out type (slashed or crossed through)	replace these characters with those marked in the margin *or* take out these characters when a take-out sign is in the margin
ringed characters	the characters are right but something needs to be changed, such as typeface or type style

Marks in the Margin	*Meaning*
written characters	add or replace where marked in the text
take-out sign (ℐ)*	take out where marked in the text
space sign (#)*	add space where marked in the text
paragraph sign (₲)*	start a new paragraph where marked in the text
close-up mark (◌)*	close up space between characters; leave no extra space
ring around instruction or description ⬭	correct the error but do not put the characters written in the ring in type

You have now learned a basic marking system that will cover nearly all errors you see. If, however, you don't know how to mark something or you forget a mark, don't panic. Just use your common sense and—

---

*These marks do not need to be put in rings because there is little danger that they will be put in type. However ⟨less #⟩ or ⟨no ₲⟩ do need rings so "less" and "no" won't be put in type.

- mark the text so it's clear where the error is;

- write in the margin either what the error is or, preferably, what to do about it. Then draw a ring around what you have written in the margin to show you are giving instructions.

SOME SPECIAL PROBLEMS

Wrong Word Division

When a word will not fit at the end of a line, it is divided with a hyphen. When you proofread, you will sometimes find word divisions that are unacceptable. Words should be divided syllable by syllable, preferably so that the first part of a division gives a clue to what the whole word is. Use a dictionary to look up word division. (But be aware that different dictionaries use different methods.)

When the word division is wrong, cross out both parts of the word in the text, and write out the whole word in the margin with hyphens at every acceptable place. Leave it up to the corrector to pick the place to divide the word; for example:

.........Simp-   Sim-pli-fied
lified Proofr-   Proof-read-ing
eading

Do not write out bad choices. Do not divide one-syllable words; for example, do not divide before *ed* in "launched." Do not make one-letter divisions: When you write out the divisions, do not put a hyphen after a one-letter first syllable or before a one-letter last syllable; for example, write out the word "imaginary" as "imag-i-nary" to be sure there will not be a hyphen after the one-letter first syllable (*i-*) or before the one-letter last syllable (*-y*).

Stet

"Stet" is a Latin word meaning "Let it stand." Use it when you mark something by mistake and want to say, "Ignore the mark; leave the copy the way it was before it was marked."

When you realize you have marked something by mistake, put dots under the mark in the text, cross out the mark in the margin, and write ⟨stet⟩ ; for example:

⟨stet⟩   ✗   proof~~readers~~ reading proof

Abbreviations or Spelled-Out Words

To replace an abbreviation, a symbol, or a numeral with the whole word, ring it in the text and use the proofreader's abbreviation ⟨sp⟩ (for spell out) in the margin, as shown:

	Proofreader's Mark	Corrected Copy
⟨sp⟩	5⟨%⟩	5 percent
⟨sp⟩	⟨U.S.⟩	United States
⟨sp⟩	⟨$1⟩	one dollar

Be sure you mark like this only when the spelled-out word is well known. Treat unfamiliar abbreviations as replacements; for example: ⟨U.K.⟩ *United Kingdom*

To replace a spelled-out word with an abbreviation, symbol, or numeral, mark as a simple replacement:

	Proofreader's Mark	Corrected Copy
6 ft. 2 in.	~~six feet two inches~~	6 ft. 2 in.
$40	~~forty dollars~~	$40

Marks for "Insurance"

Some characters or words make sense (or enough sense to cause problems) in different groupings. For example, the same letters that form "her ring" also form "herring;" the same letters that spell "alongside," also spell "a long side." These two-faced words need extra marks for "insurance" against mistakes.

Adding with Close-Up Marks

When characters must be added to the ends or beginnings of words, sometimes there is danger that they will be attached to the wrong word. For example, does the *t* in the following sentence belong at the end of "plan" or the beginning of "his"?

t He will plan his garden in the spring.

To prevent mistakes, use a close-up mark on characters that could go at either the end of one word or the beginning of another. A close-up mark on the right side means "attach this to the character on its right." For example, if you want "plan this," mark as follows:

t He will plan his garden in the spring.

A close-up mark on the left side means "attach this to the character on its left." For example, if you want "plant his," mark as follows:

t He will plan his garden in the spring.

Use close-up marks to be sure characters are attached to the right group; for example:

23/26   20 21 22 ∧3 24 25 2∧ 27 28 29

cI/cI   I II III IV V V∧ VI∧ VIII IX X

Don't use close-up marks to add characters in the middle of words or to add whole words.

Adding with Space Marks

Some additions would make sense either standing alone or attached to a word. For example, does the *a* in the following belong to "bout" to form "about" or should it stand alone to form "a bout"?

a He fought bout ten years ago.

52

When you see that an addition could go either way, closed up or with space around it, mark with either (1) a close-up mark or (2) space marks; for example:

1. *Proofreader's Mark for Closing Up*

He fought bout ten years ago.

Corrected Copy

He fought about ten years ago.

2. *Proofreader's Mark for Spaces*

He fought bout ten years ago.

Corrected Copy

He fought a bout ten years ago.

Taking Out with Close-Up or Space Marks

When characters are taken out of the middle of a word, the corrector has to decide whether to leave a space or to close up the characters that are left. Usually it's clear which way is correct; for example:

Simplirfied Proofreading

Simplifiedy Proofreading

But sometimes either way makes sense; for example, in the following, should "proofreading" be one word or two?

She found the proof reading through the newspaper.

If you need one word, combine the take-out sign with the close-up sign like this:

Proofreader's Mark

She found the proof reading through the newspaper.

Simplified Proofreading

Corrected Copy

Corrected Copy

She found the proofreading through the newspaper.

If you need two words, use the space sign to replace the *e*, like this:

Proofreader's Mark

\#   She found the proof⌿reading through the newspaper.

Corrected Copy

She found the proof reading through the newspaper.

You can use one take-out-and-close-up mark in the text for more than one character, as shown:

⌒   proof~~ing~~reading

Never use a take-out-and-close-up mark to take out a whole word or you will end up with no space between words.

Other Problems

To mark other kinds of problems, first show where the problem is in the text; next, in the margin, tell what the problem is or what to do about it and draw a ring around what you have written. Use an example if it will help. Here are some marks for other kinds of problems:

Simplified Proof(re)ading	(bad type)
Simplifi(e)d Proofr(e)ading	(clean lc e's)
(Sim pl i fi ed Pr oo freadi ng)	(uneven # between letters)
Simplified (P)roofreading	ꝗ
Simplified Proofread(in)g	(wrong type)
Now is the time	(underline)
Now is, the time	(ꝗ part of underline)

Warning About Upcoming Practice Exercises

In the exercises up to now, the lines of the new copy have begun and ended the same as the lines of the old copy. From now on the lines of new and old copy will often begin and end differently.

You need not mark to make the new copy match the old line for line. In real-life proofreading, you should let the corrector decide when to change line beginnings or endings. Also let the corrector decide when changes call for new word divisions (hyphens) at the ends of lines, and when words that were divided can be put together on one line.

PRACTICE 12. SPECIAL PROBLEMS

Follow the instructions for each part of the following practice. Check your work against the answer key in Appendix E.

A. Mark the following word divisions for correction when they are wrong:

    ......January-
    y

    ....Febr-
    uary

    ....March-
    ch

    ....A-
    pril

    ....Ju-
    ly

    ....Aug-
    ust

    ......Septem-
    ber

    ....Oc-
    tober

    ....Nov-
    ember

    ....Dece-
    mber

B. Mark the righthand column so that, when it is corrected, it will match the lefthand column:

ADM William Jones, Senior, was born in Roanoke, Va., on December 19, 1921. He received his Bachelor of Arts degree from Illinois College in 1942, the same year he joined the U.S. Navy as an ensign.	Admiral Wm. Jones, Sr., was born in Roanoke, Virginia, on Dec. 19, 1921. He received his B.A. degree from Ill. Coll. in 1942, the same year he joined the United States Navy as an ENS.

C. Mark "round" to make "around."   round

    Mark "long" to make "belong."   long

    Mark "ward" to make "award."   ward

    Mark "devil" to make "deviltry."   devil

    Mark "van" to make "vanguard."   van

    Mark "in exact" to make "inexact."   in exact

    Mark "whole sale" to make "wholesale."   whole sale

    Mark "around" to make "a round."   around

    Mark "belong" to make "be long."   belong

    Mark "award" to make "a ward."   award

    Mark "deviltry" to make "devil try."   deviltry

    Mark "vanguard" to make "van guard."   vanguard

    Mark "inexact" to make "in exact."   inexact

    Mark "wholesale" to make "whole sale."   wholesale

D. Mark the column at the right to match the column at the left.

surefire   surerfire

rolltop   rollertop

marketplace   marketingplace

cardboard   cardoboard

daydream   daysdream

field day   fieldyday

ground cover   groundscover

ice pick   icerpick

No one quality stands alone.   Noon equality stands a lone.

Among you I see half with erring Among you I see halfwit herring
ways.   ways.

Together we got her everything.   To get her we go there very thing.

PRACTICE 13. PROOFREADING REVIEW EXERCISE*

Check your work against the answer key in Appendix E.

Part 1, Adding: Proofread the column on the right, comparing it to the column on the left. Mark the righthand column to add omitted characters, words, or passages. Remember lines no longer match exactly.

ROMANCES

In ages when there were no books,
when noblemen and princes themselves
could not read, history or tradition
was monopolized by the story-tellers.
They inherited, generation after generation, the wondrous tales of their
predecessors, which they retailed to
the public with such additions of their
own as they acquired information to
supply them with. Anachronisms became
of course very common, and errors of
geography, of locality, of manners,
equally so. Spurious genealogies
were invented, in which Arthur and
his knights, and Charlemagne and his
paladins, were made to derive their
descent from Aeneas, Hector, or some
other of the Trojan heroes.

ROMANCE

In ages when there were no boks,
when noblemen themselves could not
read, histy or tradition was monopolized by the story tellers. They
inherit, generation after generation,
the tales of their predecessors,
which they retailed the public with
additions of their own as they acquired
information to supply them. Anachronisms became of course common, and errors
of geography, of manners, equally so.
Spurous genealogies were invented in
which Arthur and his nights, and
Charlemagne and his paladins, were made
to derive descent from Aeneas, Hector, or
other of the Trojan heros.

Part 2, Taking Out: Proofread the column on the right by comparing it to the column on the left. Mark the righthand column to take out any extra characters, words, or passages.

At a time when chivalry excited
universal admiration, and when all the
efforts of that chivalry were directed
against the enemies of religion, it was
natural that literature should receive
the same impulse, and that history and
fable should be ransacked to furnish
examples of courage and piety that might
excite increased emulation. Arthur and
Charlemagne were the two heroes selected
for this purpose.

At a time when chivalary excited
universal admiration, and, when all
of the efforts of that same chivalry
were directed against the enenemies
of religion, it was entirely natural
that litterature should receive the
the same impulses, and that history,
story, and fable should be ransacked
to furnish examples of courage and
to furnish examples of courage and
piety that might excite an increased
emulation. King Arthur and Charlemagne
were the two great heroes selected for
for this very purpose.

*The text for this exercise is from *Bullfinch's Mythology.*

Part 3, Replacing: Proofread the column on the right by comparing it to the column on the left. Mark for all replacements needed in characters, words, or passages, including changes of typeface or type style and transpositions. (Two ways of marking transpositions are correct. You may mark transpositions with the double loop and (tr), as on the answer keys, or you may simply mark transposed characters to be replaced with characters in the correct order.)

Arthur's pretentions were that he was a brave, though not always successing warrior, he had withheld with great resolve the army of the infidels, that is to say, of the saxons, and his menory was held in the highest estimation by his countrymen, the Britons, who carried into Wales with them, and into the kindred country of Armorica, or Brittany, the memories of his exploits, which their National vanity insensible exaggerates, until the little prince of the Silures (South Wales" was magnified into the conqueror of England, of Gaul, and of the larger part of Europe. His geneology was gradually carried up to an imaginary Brutus, and to the period of the Trojan War, and a sort of cornilce was composed in the Welch, or American, language which, under the pompous title of The History Of The Kings of Britain, was translated into Latin by Jeffery of MonMouth, about the year 1250. The Welsh critics consider the material of the work to have been an elder history, written by Saint Talian, Bishop of Asaph, in the 7th century.

Arthur's pretensions were that he was a brave, though not always successful warrior; he had withstood with great resolution the arms of the infidels, that is to say, of the Saxons, and his memory was held in the highest estimation by his countrymen, the Britons, who carried them into Wales, and into the kindred country of Armorica, or Brittany, the memory of his exploits, which their national vanity insensibly exaggerated, till the little prince of the Silures (South Wales) was magnified into the conqueror of England, of Gaul, and of the greater part of Europe. His genealogy was gradually carried up to an imaginary Brutus, and to the period of the Trojan War, and a sort of chronicle was composed in the Welsh, or Armorican, language which, under the pompous title of the History of the Kings of Britain, was translated into Latin by Geoffrey of Monmouth, about the year 1150. The Welsh critics consider the material of the work to have been an older history, written by St. Talian, Bishop of Asaph, in the seventh century.

Part 4, Adding, Taking Out, and Replacing: Proofread the column on the right, comparing it to the column on the left. Mark to add, to take out, and to replace as necessary.

As to Charlemagne, although his merits were sufficient to secure is immortalism, it was not possible that his holy wars against the Saracens should not become a farovite subject for fiction. Accordingly, the fabulous history of these wars was written, boldly ascribed to Turpin, who was Arch Bishop of Rheims about the year 773.

As to Charlemagne, though his real merits were sufficient to secure his immortality, it was impossible that his holy wars against the Saracens should not become a favorite topic for fiction. Accordingly, the fabulous history of these wars was written, probably towards the close of the eleventh century, by a monk, who, thinking it would add dignity to his work to embellish it with a contemporary name, boldly ascribed it to Turpin, who was Archbishop of Rheims about the year 773.

Part 5, Errors in Spacing and Positioning: Proofread the column on the right, comparing it to the column on the left. Mark for correction of all spacing errors and for type to be moved where necessary.

These fabulous chronicles were for awhile imprisoned in languages of local only or of professional access...The Anglo-Saxon was at that time used only by a conquered and enslaved nation...Norman Frenchalone was spoken and understood by the nobility in the greater part of Europe, and therefore was a proper vehicle for the new mode of composition. That language was Conquest, and became, after that fashionable in England before the event, the only language used at the court in London. As the various conquests of the Normans, and the enthusiastic valor of that extraordinary people, had familiarized the minds of men with the most marvellous events, their poets eagerly seized the fabulous legends of Arthur and Charlemagne, (and) translated them into the language of the day.

These fabulous chronicles were for a while imprisoned in languages of local only or of professional access... The Anglo-Saxon was at that time used only by a conquered and enslaved nation...Norman French alone was spoken and understood by the nobility in the greater part of Europe, and therefore was a proper vehicle for the new mode of composition. That language was fashionable in England before the Conquest, and became, after that event, the only language used at the court in London. As the various conquests of the Normans, and the enthusiastic valor of that extraordinary people, had familiarized the minds of men with the most marvellous events, their poets eagerly seized the fabulous legends of Arthur and Charlemagne, (and) translated them into the language of the day.

Part 6, All Kinds of Errors: Proofread the column on the right, comparing it to the column on the left. Mark for all errors in type and spacing.

METRICAL ROMANCES

The earliest from in which romances
appear is a rude kind of verse. In
In this form itis supposed they were
sung or recited at the feasts of princes
and knights inside their baronial halls.
The following specimen of the language
and style of Robert De Beauvais, who
flourished in 1527, is from Sir Walter
Scotts introduction to the Romance of
Sir Tristam.

"Ne voil pas enmi dire,
  Ici diverse la matyere..."

"I will not say to much about it,
  So diverse is the matter..."

This is a specimen of the language in
use among the mobility of England in the
ages inmediately after the Norman Conquest.
The following is a speciman of the English
that existed at the same time among the
common people. Robert de Brunne, speak=
ing of his Latin and French authorities,
says:

"Als thai haf wryten and sayt
Haf I alle in myn Inglis layd
In simple speeche as I couthe,
That is lightest in manne's mouthe.
All for the luf of symple men,
That strange Inglis cannot ken."

The "strange Inglis" being the language
of the pre vious specimen.

METRICAL ROMANCES

The earliest form in which romances
appear is that of a rude kind of verse.
In this form it is supposed they were
sung or recited at the feasts of princes
and knights in their baronial halls. The
following specimen of the language and
style of Robert de Beauvais, who flourished in 1257, is from Sir Walter Scott's
Introduction to the Romance of Sir
Tristram.

"Ne voil pas emmi dire,
  Ici diverse la matyere..."

"I will not say too much about it,
  So diverse is the matter..."

This is a specimen of the language
which was in use among the nobility of
England in the ages immediately after the
Norman conquest. The following is a
specimen of the English that existed at
the same time among the common people.
Robert de Brunne, speaking of his Latin
and French authorities, says:--

"Als thai haf wryten and sayd
Haf I alle in myn Inglis layd,
In symple speeche as I couthe,
That is lightest in manne's mouthe.
Alle for the luf of symple men,
That strange Inglis cannot ken."

The "strange Inglis" being the language
of the previous specimen.

61

COPY ERRORS AND QUERYING

Two Kinds of Error

It is important to compare the old version of what you are proofreading with the new, especially if the new version has been typewritten or typeset in its final form. You must detect and distinguish between two broad kinds of error:

- *Typesetter's or typist's errors* include any unauthorized differences between the new copy and the old and any instances of instructions not being followed.

- *Copy errors* include errors made by the writer or editor in the old version and reproduced in the new version. Copy errors are not the typesetter's or typist's fault.

You are expected to catch and mark all typesetter's or typist's errors. Copy errors are different. Professional proofreaders do not usually mark copy errors for correction; they query—write questions about them. (How to write queries is explained later.) What *you* should do about copy errors depends on a lot of things.

You should know that printing and typesetting houses and typing services absorb the cost of correcting typesetter's or typist's errors. But they charge their customers for correcting copy errors. Seemingly small things, such as changing one letter or inserting a comma, can cost as much as $50, depending on the typing or typesetting method. A change that seems minor can actually be major: adding or taking out a word may mean that a whole line must be redone; when the line spills over, a whole paragraph may be involved; if the paragraph continues on the next page, an entire page may need to be changed. The number of copy errors corrected after typing or typesetting directly affects the size of the bill and the speed of the job.

When you are proofreading, ask yourself these questions before you mark copy errors for corrections: Do I have the authority to spend the extra money? Is it worth it? Will the extra time mean a missed deadline? If I don't have the authority, whom do I ask about changes?

If you are the author and the copy is in its final form, this is obviously no time to rewrite anything. If you must make changes, try to rewrite so that no more than the affected words or lines have to be redone. Add as many characters or lines as you take out. Take out as many as you add. Replace with the same number of characters or lines as were there before.

If you are not the author, you should probably query the copy errors you consider blatant.

How to Query

Before you query, first be sure that queries will be welcome. If so, be sure that your queries are the kind that will be welcome. This is a matter of experience and judgment. As a broad rule, do not nitpick and do not edit. Query only things that would greatly puzzle a reader or seriously embarrass the author or the publisher.

When you find a copy error you think important enough to query, either underline it or mark a pointer in the text and then, in the margin, write a brief question followed by a question mark in a ring. The idea is that the author or editor— the person who goes over the copy after you—can cross out the whole query if it's not acceptable. If the suggestion is acceptable, just the question mark will be deleted, changing the query to a marked correction.

Here are some examples of proper queries:

1492 (?)
ocean blue (?)

As the child's rhyme goes, "In 1493, Columbus sailed the deep blue sea."

affected (?)
squeegee (?)

With a contoured wood handle that allows long use without muscle strain, and a top-quality rubber blade that is not effected by oils, benzine, varnishes, or lacquer, our sqeegee is the best on the market.

We pride ourselves on a quality product and a far price. *i* (?)

WORKING WITH A PARTNER OR ALONE

Working with a Partner

For non-professionals, proofreading with a partner is very much more accurate than proofreading alone. In a partnership, one person reads aloud from the older version while the other follows the newer copy and marks it for correction.

Reading Aloud

If you are the one who reads aloud, you must indicate everything to your partner, including the following:

- Every word, spelling out any that could be misspelled (such as people's names)

- Every punctuation mark

- Every paragraph and any other change in spacing

- Every capital letter and any other change in type style, typeface, or type size.

You might work out some signals and shortcuts with your partner, but you must be sure your partner understands everything you do or say and, of course, everything you agree not to say. For example, you might decide to shorten words like comma (and say "com") or semicolon (and say "sem"). You might decide not to indicate the capital letter that begins a sentence. Many such shortcuts are possible with partners who work together a lot.

Marking

If you are the partner doing the marking, you have to be good at spelling. You must look not just at words, but at individual characters, or you will miss errors. You must also look at pages as a whole, or you will miss errors in spacing.

Working Alone

When you proofread alone, comparing the old version with the new, take special care to catch omissions and unwanted repetitions. They are easy to miss for one pair of eyes skipping back and forth between the two versions. It doesn't hurt to read aloud to yourself.

TIPS AND CAUTIONS

- Be sure to read instructions or specifications carefully before you start work.

- Always check the page numbers of both the older and the newer copy. You will save yourself grief if you learn before you start proofreading that pages are missing or out of order.

- Don't skip anything. Read every character, every heading, every page number. On a letter, read the complimentary close and the list of enclosures.

- Be especially careful when you start or finish a stint of work, or after an interruption. Proofreaders seem to miss errors at these times.

- Be extra careful with the first title or headline, the first sentence, the first paragraph, and the first page; these are places where uncaught errors are especially noticeable to readers of the finished document and embarrassing to the publisher.

- Watch carefully for errors in words that appear in headlines, all caps, italic, boldface, or small type. These errors are easier to miss than those in normal type.

- When you find an error, watch for another nearby. Errors often come in groups.

- Try looking at pages upside down and sideways. This may help you see spacing errors.

- Watch characters that belong in pairs. Sometimes a closing parenthesis or a closing quotation mark is missing.

- Take special care with numbers, such as dollar amounts, figures in tables, and dates; a missed error could be disastrous.

- Double check any sequence of numbers or letters. Alphabetical order is sometimes mixed up. Numbered or lettered lists, paragraphs, or footnotes sometimes skip or repeat a number or letter, for example: 1235, abce.

- Be sure there are footnotes on the page to match every footnote reference in the text.

- Check the page numbers in a table of contents or a list of illustrations against the text pages to be sure they are right. Check the titles, too, to be sure they match.

- Use a soft, erasable, black or bright colored pencil. Do not use ink.

- If you see more than five or six broken or defective characters on a proof from a typesetter, see if the typesetter will provide another proof. Do not clutter the margin with many bad type marks; they are confusing to the corrector, who could then easily miss another kind of mark. If necessary, write a general note; for example: "Many bad c's and o's."

- Watch for any kind of recurring error or query. If the same kind of thing happens over and over, write a general note instead of marking every instance, for example: "summer time and summertime: both appear throughout. Which is right?" or "chapter heads sometimes centered, sometimes not. OK?" Better yet, if you can, ask the author or editor for a decision about frequent queries. Then you can mark correctly as you go.

- Be sure to check corrections carefully. The probability of new errors being introduced in the process of correction is astonishingly high.

Spelling

If you are not perfect at spelling, learn which words you don't know and look them up every time you come across them. Here is a list of words often uncorrected when wrong; do not let any slip past you.

accommodate (2 c's, 2 m's)
acknowledgment (no e)*
affect, effect (see next paragraph)
capital, capitol (see next paragraph)
changeable
commitment, committed, committing
computer
conscience
consensus
coolly
deductible
defendant
dependent
drunkenness
embarrass
engineering
foreword (front of a book; remember the word *before*)
harass
hypocrisy
inadvertent
indispensable
irresistible
judgment (no e)*
liaison
manageable
necessary
occurrence, occurred, occurring
parallel
permissible
Pittsburgh, Pa. (but Pittsburg, Kans., Okla., Calif., and Texas)
prairie
precede, preceding
principal, principle
principally (see next paragraph)
privilege
proceed, proceeding
publicly
receive
recommend
resistance
seize
separate
siege
sizable*
supersede
totally
vacuum
weird
wholly

*Although Merriam-Webster dictionaries give a second spelling with an *e*, this should usually be changed.

Learn the differences between frequently confused words:

- *Affect, effect.* "To affect" means "to influence." Effect means "result"; "to effect" means "to result in."

- *Capital, capitol.* The only time the word gets an *o* is when it means a government building (usually one with a d*o*me).

- *Principal, principle.* Princip*a*l (with an *a*) means "m*a*in." As an *a*djective, the word is always spelled with an *a*. A princip*a*l is a chief (a m*a*in person). A princip*le* (with an *le*) is a ru*le* or a proposition.

Checking

It is often wise to follow proofreading with a checking step. To check, scan the new version, paying special attention to the things listed in the section on tips and cautions.

For a thorough check, read the new version sentence by sentence.

Knowing the Job

Suit the level of work to the document. An informal memo to the manager downstairs may need nothing more than a quick scan of the new version. A contract or a budget may need several two-person proofreadings and checkings.

Be sure you know what is expected of you. Are you supposed to make corrections or only to query?

Find out if you are expected to check arithmetic (such as the addition of numbers in tables); to look up quotations to be sure they are accurate; to do the research to see that a book's author, title, and publisher are cited correctly in a bibliography; or to verify the accuracy of dates or the spelling of people's names.

Find out if you are expected to catch inconsistencies in style. "Style" in this sense concerns such choices as the following:

- capitals: the manager *or* the Manager

- abbreviations: Fri. *or* Fr. *or* F.

- commas in a series of words: A, B, and C *or* A, B and C

- numbers: 16 people *or* sixteen people

- compound words: summer time *or* summer-time *or* summertime.

Is there a style guide you are supposed to follow? Organizations that prefer not to leave style decisions to individual writers may specify a style guide or put out one of their own. Style manuals often used include *Words Into Type* (Prentice-Hall), *A Manual of Style* (University of Chicago Press), *U.S. Government Printing Office Style Manual* (Superintendent of Documents, Washington, D.C. 20402), and newspaper or press service guides.

Proofreading marks are instructions. Instructions must make sense. Whatever you proofread, you should understand what will happen next. Find out how the type was produced, how corrections will be made, and where the copy you are reading fits into the production process. For example, among the many things you should know are the following:

If you read galley proofs, you should understand that they have not yet been divided into pages. Footnotes, and sometimes headings, are out of order; illustrations are often not shown.

If you read "camera-ready copy," you should understand that the camera will not see the page as you do or perhaps as your photocopying machine does. For example, the camera will not detect pale blue marks, cut-in "windows," or white tape.

If you read copy from a phototypesetting machine, you should know that a block of type that looks too faint or too bold should probably be marked "check density" and not "wrong type."

REVIEW OF SIMPLIFIED PROOFREADING

General Rules

Every error gets two marks: (1) a mark in the line of type (the text) to show where to make a correction and (2) a mark in the margin to show what is wrong or what to do at the point marked in the text.

Slashes separate two or more marks in the margin.

Marks in the margin go from left to right.

Marks in the left margin are for errors in the left side of the text. Marks in the right margin are for errors in the right side of the text.

Special Symbols and Abbreviations

#	space
⌐	take out
¶	paragraph
⌒	move characters together; leave no extra space
( )	(ring around instruction or description): take care of the error but do not type or set the characters inside the ring
(Cap)	capital letter
(lc)	lowercase letter
(Caps + lc)	caps and lowercase (usually initial caps)
⌐̂	take out and then move the remaining characters together
(sp)	spell out abbreviation, numeral, or symbol

71

Proofreader's Marks

Action Needed	*Marks in Text*	*Marks in Margin*	*Meaning*	*Corrected Copy*
Add	abc d̠f ghi	e	add e between d and f	abc def ghi
	abc xyz	to	add to	abc to xyz
	123 789	456	add 456 be-tween lines	123 456 789
	abc̠def ghi	#	add space	abc def ghi
	123 456 789	#	add space between lines	123 456 789
Take Out or Replace				
single letters	abc de∦f ghi	ℐ	take out y	abc def ghi
	abc d∦f ghi	e	replace y with e	abc def ghi
multiple letters	abc ~~xyz~~ def ghi	ℐ	take out xyz	abc def ghi
	abc ~~xyz~~ ghi	def	replace xyz with def	abc def ghi
Change Typeface or Type Style	Ⓐbc def ghi	(lc)	change cap to lowercase	abc def ghi
	ⓐBC DEF GHI	(cap)	change lower-case to cap	ABC DEF GHI
	(abc def ghi)	(italic)	change roman to italic	*abc def ghi*

72

Action Needed	Marks in Text	Marks in Margin	Meaning	Corrected Copy
Change Spacing or Position of Type	a͡bc def ghi	͡	close up space; leave no space	abc def ghi
	abc ⌒ def ghi	_less #_	less space	abc def ghi
	abc d^e$_f$ ghi	_align_	align	abc def ghi
	|123 456 7|89	_align_	align	123 456 789
	123 ⌐456 789	_move left_	move left	123 456 789
	⌐ abc ⌐	_center_	center	abc
Special Problems	word ~~divisi-~~ ~~on~~	di - vi - sion	correct wrong word division	word divi-sion
	abc ~~def~~ ghi	✗ (_stet_)	let it stand as it was before marks were made	abc def ghi
	ab∧ def ghi	͡ ͡	add character closed up to its left	abc def ghi
	ab c de ∧ gh i	# f #	add character with space at both sides	ab c de f gh i
	ab⸸c def ghi	⸝	take out and close up remaining characters	abc def ghi
	abc⸸def ghi	#	take out and leave space	abc def ghi
Other Problems	Mark the place	Tell what's wrong or how to fix it. Draw a ring around the words.		

FINAL NOTE

You now know the whole Simplified Proofreading System.

You know what kinds of errors to look for. You know how to make basic proofreading marks and how to mark anything the basic marks don't take care of.

Now you have to be sure that the person making the corrections understands your marks. If that person knows proofreading marks, you have no problem. If the corrector does not know the marks, just hand over this book. Point out that ten minutes' study of the Summary on the inside back cover will explain just about everything you have done.

Of course, the corrector can learn all the ins and outs of Simplified Proofreading as you did—by working through a copy of this book.

PRACTICE 14. FINAL EXERCISE

To make this exercise more like real-life proofreading, it differs from the others in two ways: (1) There are two pages instead of two columns to compare. (2) The old version has editor's marks.

Compare the following pages. Mark the page labeled "new version" so that, when it is corrected, it will match the page labeled "old version" exactly, including the changes the editor has written in. Mark in both margins.

When you are finished, compare your marks to those in the answer key in Appendix E.

Simplified Proofreading

Old Version
PROVERBS FOR PROOFREADING

Type in letter gothic   *Put in 2 columns*

¶ Love is *nearsighted* ~~blind~~. When you are the writer, editor, typist, or typesetter proofreading your own work, you will almost surely suffer from myopia. You are too close to see all the errors. *Get help.* ¶ Familiarity breeds content. When you see the same copy again and again through the different stages of production and revision, you may *well* miss new errors. Fresh eyes are needed. ¶ If it's as plain as the nose on your face, everybody can see it but you. Where is the reader most likely to notice errors? In a headline; in a title; in the first line, first paragraph, or first page of copy; and in the top lines of a new page. These are precisely the places where editors and proofreaders are most likely to miss errors. Take extra care at every beginning. ¶ Mistakery loves company. Errors *often* ~~frequently~~ cluster. When you find one, look hard for others nearby. ¶ When you change horses in midstream, you can get wet. It's easy to overlook an error set in type that is different from the text face you are reading. Watch out when type changes to all caps, italics, boldface, small sizes, and large sizes. Watch out when underlines appear in typewritten copy. ¶ Glass houses invite stones. Beware copy that discusses errors. When the subject is typographical quality, the copy must be *typographically* perfect. When the topic is errors in grammar or spelling, the copy must be error-free. Keep alert for words like typographical or proofreading. Double check and triple check. ¶ The footbone conneckit to the kneebone? Numerical and alphabetical sequences often go awry. Check for omissions and duplications in footnote numbers, page numbers, or notations in outlines and lists. Check any numeration, anything in alphabetical order, and everything sequential (such as the path of arrows in a flowchart). ¶ It takes two to boogie. An opening parenthesis needs ~~needs~~ a closing parenthesis. Brackets, quotation marks, and sometimes dashes belong in pairs. Catch the bachelors. ¶ Every yoohoo deserves a yoohoo back. A footnote reference mark or a first reference to a table or an illustration is termed a callout. Be sure a footnote begins on the same page as its callout. Be sure a table or illustration follows its callout as soon as possible. ¶ Numbers can speak louder than words. Misprints in numerals (figures) can be catastrophic. Take extraordinary care with dollar figures and numbers in dates, statistics, tables, or technical text. Read all numerals character by character; for example, read "1979" as "one nine seven nine." Be sure any figures in your *hand* writing are unmistakable. ¶ Two plus two is twenty-two. The simplest math can go wrong. Do not trust figures giving percentages and fractions or the "total" lines in tables. Watch *for misplaced* ~~the~~ d*e*cimal points. Use your calculator. ¶ Above all, never assume that all is well. As the saying goes, ass-u-me makes an ass out of u and me.

76

New Version

PROVERBS FOR PROOFREADERS

Love is nearsighted. When you are the writer, editor, typist or typesetter proofreading your own work, you will almost surely suffer from myopia. You are too close to see all the errors. Get help.

Familiarity breeds content. When you see the same copy again and again through the different stages of production and revision, you may well miss new errors. Fresh eyes are needed.

If it's as plain as the nose on your face, everbody can see it but you. Where is the reader most likely to notice errors? In a headline; in a title; in the first line, first paragraph, or first page of copy; and in the top lines of a new page. These are precisely the places where editors and proofreaders are very likely to miss errors. Take extra care at every beginning.

Mistakery loves company. Errors often cluster. When you find one, look hard for others near by.

When you change horses in midstream, you can get wet. It's easy to overlook an error set in type that is different from the text face you are reading. Watch out when type changes to all caps, italics, boldface, small sizes, and large sizes. Watch out when umderlines appear in typewritten copy.

Glass houses invite stones. Beware copy that discusses errors. When the subject is typographical quality, the copy must be typographically perfect. When the topic is errors in grammar or spelling, the copy must be error-free. Keep alert for words like typograhical or proofreading. Double check and triple check.

The footbone conneckit to the kneebone? Numerical and alphabetical sequences often go awry. Check for omissions and duplications in page numbers, footnote numbers, or notations in outlines and lists. Check any enumeration, anything in alphabetical order, and everything sequential (such as as the path of arrows in a flowchart)

It takes two to boogie. An opening parenthesis needs a closing parenthesis. Brackets, quotation marks, and sometimes dashes, belong in pairs. Catch the bachelors.

Every yoohoo deserves a yoohoo back. A footnote reference mark or a first reference to a table of an illlustraton is termed a callout. Be sure a footnote begins on the same page as its callout. Be sure a table or illustration follows its callout as soon as possible.

Numbers can speak louder than words. Misprints in numerals (figures) can be catastropnic. Take extraordinary care with dollar figures and numbers in dates, statistics, tables, or technical text. Read all numerals character by character; for example, read "1979" as "one nine seven nine." Be sure any figures in your hand writing are unmistakable.

Two plus two is twenty-two. The simplest math can go wrong. Do not trust figures giving percentages and fractions or the "total" lines in tables. Watch for misplaced decimal points. Use your calculator.

Above all, never assume that all is well. As the saying goes, ass-u-me makes an ass cut of u an me.

APPENDIX A. SAMPLE CORRECTION LIST

The sample, handwritten correction list on the next page shows the same corrections marked on the Example of Simplified Proofreader's Marks on the inside back cover.

A correction list must indicate by number the page, paragraph, and line involved, must pinpoint where the error is in a line, and must tell what to do about the error. The column labeled "Error in Text" corresponds to the proofreading marks made in the text. The column labeled "Correction" corresponds to the marks made in the margin.

Page	Para	Line	Error in Text	Correction
In-side back cover	1	1	wrong spacing	(move line left)
			Wi/\liam	l
			Berkeley /\	(comma)
		2	Virginia /\	from 1642
		4-5	wrong spacing betw lines	(add #)
		6	day, ~~in his famous statmt~~	S
		7	statement ,"/\	(add #)
		8-9	wrong spacing betw lines	(less #)
		9	printing ;/	(comma)
		10	w/\ell	i
		11	~~too~~	hundred
			~~education~~	learning
		12	~~braohght~~	brought
		12,13	he-resy	her-esy
		14	prin t n g	(align)
		15	and ⌒ libels	(less #)
		16	(G)overnment	(lc)
		17-18	both." (Berkeley	(same line)
		18	erro(r)	(bad letter)
		19	had ~~existed~~	(3 part of underline)
		20	wrong spacing	(move line right to align)
		21	Klapper ①	(superscript 1)
	footnote 1		[1] ter	(move down)
		2	Williamsburg	(underline)

APPENDIX B. PROFESSIONAL PROOFREADING MARKS FOR PUNCTUATION AND SYMBOLS

ampersand (&)

at sign (@)

apostrophe (')

asterisk (*)

brackets

 opening bracket -- [

 closing bracket --]

colon (:)

comma (,)

dash (see box at right)

dollar sign ($)

exclamation point (!)

hyphen (-)

minus sign (-)

number sign (#)

parentheses

 opening parenthesis -- (

 closing parenthesis --)

period (.)

plus sign (+)

question mark (?)

quotation marks

 opening single quote (')

Typewritten Copy Only

=/ short dash (equivalent to en dash)

--/ long dash (equivalent to em dash)

Typeset Copy Only

$\frac{1}{N}$ en dash

$\frac{1}{M}$ em dash

$\frac{2}{M}$ 2-em dash

---

closing single quote (')

opening double quote (")

closing double quote (")

semicolon (;)

subscript

 for example, mark H_2O to get H_2O

superscript

 for example, mark $3^2 = 9$ to get $3^2 = 9$

Mark other symbols with their names in a ring, for example:

α (Greek alpha)

TYPEWRITER LINES		
1		1
2		2
3		3
4		4
5		5
6	1 in	6
7		7
8		8
9		9
10		10
11		11
12	2 in	12
13		13
14		14
15		15
16		16
17		17
18	3 in	18
19		19
20		20
21		21
22		22
23		23
24	4 in	24
25		25
26		26
27		27
28		28
29		29
30	5 in	30
31		31
32		32
33		33
34		34
35		35
36	6 in	36
37		37
38		38
39		39
40		40
41		41
42	7 in	42
43		43
44		44
45		45
46		46
47		47
48	8 in	48

APPENDIX C. RULERS FOR TYPEWRITTEN COPY

12-pitch (Elite)
character ruler

10-pitch (Pica)
character ruler

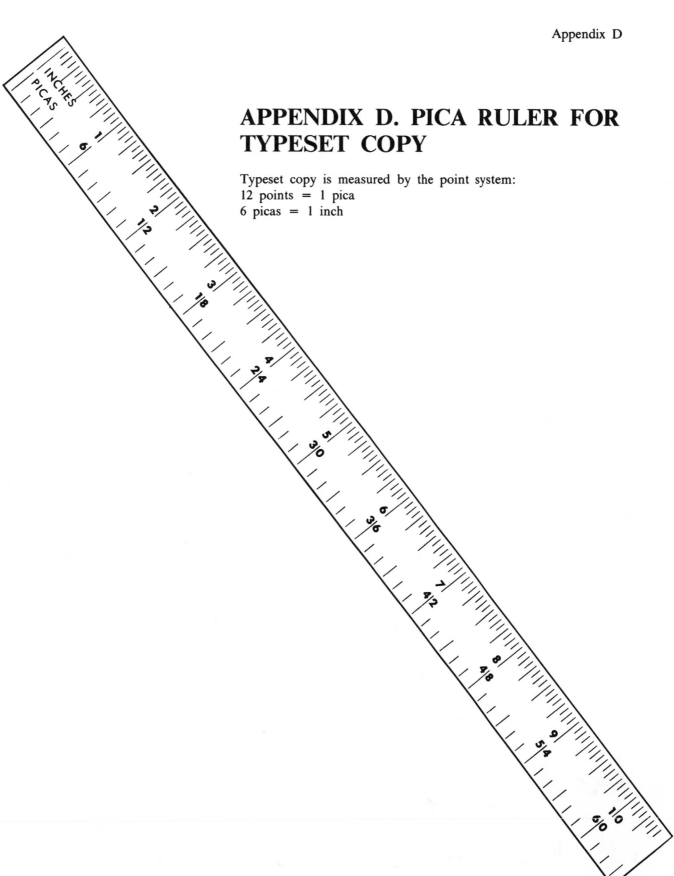

APPENDIX D. PICA RULER FOR TYPESET COPY

Typeset copy is measured by the point system:
12 points = 1 pica
6 picas = 1 inch

APPENDIX E. ANSWER KEYS TO EXERCISES

PRACTICE 2. TAKING OUT TYPE, ANSWER KEY

Compare the column on the left below to the column on the right. Mark the righthand column so that, when corrections are made, it will match the lefthand column exactly.

1234567890

12374567890

abcdefghijklmnopqrstuvwxyz

abxcdefghijkylmnopqrstxuvwxyz

1970	1970
1971	1971ø
1972	1972
1973	1973
1974	~~1969~~
1975	1974
1976	1975
1977	1976
1978	1977
1979	1978
	øß 1979

Thirty days hath September,
April, June, and November.
All the rest have thirty-one
Save February, which alone
Has twenty-eight,
  and one day more
Is added to each year in four.

Thirtyy days hath September,
April, ~~May,~~ June, and November.
All the rest have thirty-oney
Save ~~Feb~~ February, which alone
Has twenty-eight,
  and one day more
Is added to each yearø in four.

Life is our dictionary. . . .
Life lies behind us as the
quarry from whence we get
tiles and copestones for the
masonry of today. This is
the way to learn grammar.
Colleges and books only copy
the language which the field
and the work-yard made.
                Ralph Waldo Emerson
                The American Scholar

Life is ¢our dictionary. . . .
Life lies ~~right~~ behind us as the
quarry from whence we get
tiles and copestones for the
masonary of today. This is
the way to learn grammar.
Colleges and books only ~~just~~ copy
the language which the field
and ~~also~~ the work-yard made.
              ~~by~~ Ralph Waldo Emerson
              ~~in~~ The American Scholar

PRACTICE 3. ADDING TYPE, ANSWER KEY

Compare the column on the left below to the column on the right. Mark the righthand column so that, when corrections are made, it will match the lefthand column exactly.

1234567890

abcdefghijklmnopqrstuvwxyz

1970
1971
1972
1973
1974
1975
1976
1977
1978
1979

4 123567890

b/k acdefghijlmnopqrsuvwxyz *t*

1970
1972 1971
1973
1974
1975
7 196
1977
1978
1 979

Thirty days hath September,
April, June, and November.
All the rest have thirty-one
Save February, which alone
Has twenty-eight,
   and one day more
Is added to each year in four.

Life is our dictionary. . . .
Life lies behind us as the
quarry from whence we get
tiles and copestones for the
masonry of today. This is
the way to learn grammar.
Colleges and books only copy
the language which the field
and the work-yard made.
        Ralph Waldo Emerson
        The American Scholar

p Thirty days hath September, *and*
Aril, June, November.
All the rest have thirty-ne *o*
February Save, which alone
y/i Has twent-eght,
   and one day more
Is added to each yer in four. *a*

c Life is our ditionary. . . .
Life lies behind as the *us*
m quarry fro whence we get
c tiles and copstones for the
r masony of today. This is
the way to learn. *grammar only*
l Coleges and books copy
which the language the field *d*
and the work-yar made.
Ralph Waldo Emerson
        The American Scholar

86

PRACTICE 4. TAKING OUT AND ADDING TYPE, ANSWER KEY

Compare the column on the left below to the column on the right. Mark the righthand column for adding and taking out, so that, when corrections are made, it will match the lefthand column exactly.

Left column	Mark	Right column	Mark
We all know that as the	*all*	We know that ~~just~~ as the	S
human body can be nourished	S / S	human/ body can~~not~~ be nourished	
on any food, though it were	S	on any food, /Although	*it were*
boiled grass and the broth		boiled grass and the broth	
of shoes, so the human mind	S	of ~~old~~ shoes, so the human mind	
can be fed by any knowledge.	S	can be fed by ~~fled by~~ any knowledge.	
And great and heroic men	S	And ~~many~~ great and heroicll men	S
have existed who had almost	*existed who*	have had almost	
no other information than by		no other information/ than by	S
the printed page. I would	*the / S*	printed page/. I would	
only say that it needs a	S	only say that ~~surely~~ it needs a	
strong head to bear that diet.	S	~~very~~ strong head that diet.	*to bear*

PRACTICE 5. REPLACING WRONG CHARACTERS WITH RIGHT ONES, ANSWER KEY

Compare the column on the left below to the column on the right. Mark the righthand column so that, when corrections are made, it will match the lefthand column exactly.

```
1234567890                              3    12∮4567890

abcdefghijklmnopqrstuvwxyz      c/l    abⅹdefghijk∤mnopqrs∤uvwxyz      t

1970                                         1970
1971                                    1    197∮
1972                                         1972
1973                                         1973
1974                                         1974
1975                                         1975
1976                                    76   194̸4̸
1977                                         1977
1978                                         1978
1979                               1979  2001
```

```
Thirty days hath September,                 Thirty days hath July,           September
April, June, and November.          u       April, Jαne, and November.
All the rest have thirty-one        have    All the rest number thirty-one
Save February, which alone       February   Save Saturday, which alone
Has twenty-eight,                   e       Has twαnty-eight,
  and one day more                            and one day more
Is added to each year in four.              Is added to every one in four.   each year


Life is our dictionary. . . .               Life is our encyclopedia. . . .    dictionary
Life lies behind us as the                  Life lies ahead of us as the       behind
quarry from whence we get                   quarry from whence we acquire       get
tiles and copestones for the                tiles and copestones for the
masonry of today.  This is       masonry    bricklaying of today.  This is
the way to learn grammar.     the way to    how we learn grammar.
Colleges and books only copy                Colleges and schools only copy     books
the language which the field                the language which the laborers    field
and the work-yard made.          and        in the work-yard made.
        Ralph Waldo Emerson                         Ralph Frodo Emerson        Waldo
        The American Scholar                        The American Scholar
```

PRACTICE 6 (OPTIONAL). TRANSPOSING, ANSWER KEY

Do this exercise if you want to practice using the special marks for transposing. Compare the column on the left to the column on the right. Mark corrections in the righthand column with the double loop in the text and ⟨tr⟩ in the margin.

1. Mark "houseboat" to make "boathouse."   houseboat ⟨tr⟩

2. Mark "racehorse" to make "horserace."   racehorse ⟨tr⟩

3. Mark "songbird" to make "birdsong."   songbird ⟨tr⟩

4. Mark "silver coin" to make "coin silver."   silver coin ⟨tr⟩

5. Mark "human being" to make "being human."   human being ⟨tr⟩

6. Mark "How is she wrong?" to make "How wrong is she?"   How is she wrong? ⟨tr⟩

7. Mark "lien" to make "line."   lien ⟨tr⟩

8. Mark "trail" to make "trial."   trail ⟨tr⟩

9. Mark "silver" to make "sliver."   silver ⟨tr⟩

10. Mark "barn" to make "bran."   barn ⟨tr⟩

11. Mark "casual" to make "causal."   casual ⟨tr⟩

12. Mark "stake" to make "takes."   stake ⟨tr⟩

13. Mark "sword" to make "words."   sword ⟨tr⟩

14. Mark "procede" to make "proceed."   procede ⟨tr⟩

15. Mark "bear" to make "bare."   bear ⟨tr⟩

15. Mark "grate" to make "great."   grate ⟨tr⟩

17. Mark "ware" to make "wear."   ware ⟨tr⟩

18. Mark "seat" to make "sate."   seat ⟨tr⟩

19. Mark "bake" to make "beak."   bake ⟨tr⟩

20. Mark "aide" to make "idea."   aide ⟨tr⟩

21. Mark "range to make "anger."   range ⟨tr⟩

PRACTICE 7. TAKING OUT, ADDING, AND REPLACING TYPE, ANSWER KEY

Compare the column on the left below to the column on the right. Mark the righthand column so that, when corrections are made, it will match the lefthand column exactly.

Over the office door of Aldus	Over ~~Above~~ the office door of Aldus
Manutius (1450-1515), founder	1450 Manutius (~~1540~~-1515), founder
of the Aldine Press in Venice,	i/e of the Alden Press in Venice,
appeared this legend: Whoever	legend appeared this ~~motto:~~ Whoever
you are, you are earnestly re-	are you ~~may be~~, you are earnesly re-
quested by Aldus to state your	quested by Aldus to state your
business briefly and to take	u bsiness briefly and to take
your departure promptly. In	departure your ~~leave~~ promptly. In
this way you may be of service	way this ~~manner~~ you may service
even as was Hercules to the	was even as ~~did~~ Hercules to the
weary Atlas, for this is a	weary Atlas for this is a
place of work for everyone who	k place of worship for everyone who
enters.	s enter.

PRACTICE 8. CHANGING TYPEFACE AND TYPE STYLE, ANSWER KEY

Compare the column on the left below to the column on the right. Mark the righthand column so that, when corrections are made, it will match the lefthand column exactly.

WORDS ABOUT WORDS

Epigrams

A powerful agent is the
right word.
—*Mark Twain*

Longer than deeds liveth
the word.
—*Pindar*

Be not the slave
of words.
—*Carlyle*

Words are stubborn things.
—*Zartman*

Words make love.
—*Andre Breton*

A word, once sent abroad,
flies irrevocably.
—*Horace*

People who say they love
words are the biggest
bores of all.
—*Minor*

Words pay no debts.
—*Shakespeare*

Syllables govern the world.
—*John Selden*

Words About Words — *italic / all caps*

Epigrams — *boldface roman*

A powerful agent is the
right word.
—Mark Twain — *italic*

*Longer than deeds liveth
the word.*
—P*INDAR* — *roman / lc*

Be not the slave
of words.
—*Carlyle*

Words are stubborn things. — *roman*
—Zartman — *italic*

WORDS MAKE LOVE. — *regular cap + lc*
—**Andre Breton** — *italic*

A Word, Once Sent Abroad,
Flies Irrevocably. — *all lc*
—*Horace*

People who say they love
words are the biggest
bores of all.
—*Minor*

Words pay no debts.
—**Shakespeare** — *italic*

Syllables govern the world.
—*John Selden*

91

PRACTICE 9. REVIEW OF MARKS, ANSWER KEY

Do the following exercises, marking as efficiently as possible.

1. Take away from "now" to make "no."   no~~w~~   ⌇

2. Take away from "there" to make "here."   ⌇   ~~t~~here

3. Take away from "pencil" to make "pen."   pen~~cil~~   ⌇

4. Take away from "grandchild" to make "child."   ⌇   ~~grand~~child

5. Take away from "friend" to make "fiend."   ⌇   f~~r~~iend

6. Take away from "exist" to make "exit."   ⌇   exi~~s~~t

7. Take away from "display" to make "play."   ⌇   ~~dis~~play

8. Take away from "proofread" to make "read."   ⌇   ~~proof~~read

9. Take away from "bellow" to make "below."   ⌇   bel~~l~~ow

10. Take away from "language" to make "age."   ⌇   ~~langu~~age

11. Take away from "complete" to make "compete."   ⌇   comp~~l~~ete

12. Take away from "whole" to make "hole."   ⌇   ~~w~~hole

13. Add to "no" to make "now."   no⌄   w

14. Add to "here" to make "there."   t   ⌄here

15. Add to "pen" to make "pencil."   pen⌄   cil

16. Add to "child" to make "grandchild."   grand   ⌄child

17. Add to "fiend" to make "friend."   r   ⌄fiend

18. Add to "exit" to make "exist."   exi⌄t   s

19. Add to "play" to make "display."   dis   ⌄play

20. Add to "read" to make "proofread."   proof   ⌄read

92

21. Add to "below" to make "bellow."   below *l*

22. Add to "age" to make "language."   *langu* ‸age

23. Add to "compete" to make "complete."   compete *l*

24. Add to "hole" to make "whole."   *w* ‸hole

25. Replace "sensible" with "sensibly."   sensibl~~e~~ *y*

26. Replace "unto" with "into."   *i* ~~u~~nto

27. Replace "type" with "typical."   typ~~e~~ *ical*

28. Replace "borrow" with "tomorrow."   *tom* ~~b~~orrow

29. Replace "use" with "usage."   us~~e~~ *age*

30 Replace "survey" with "surveillance."   surve~~y~~ *illance*

31. Replace "scholar" with "scholastic."   schola~~r~~ *stic*

32. Replace "father" with "mother."   *mo* ~~fa~~ther

33. Replace "near" with "far."   *f* ~~ne~~ar

34. Replace "exercise" with "exorcise."   *o* ex~~e~~rcise

35. Replace "flour" with "flower."   flo~~u~~r   *we*

36. Replace "deported" with "reported."   *r* ~~de~~ported

Simplified Proofreading

PRACTICE 10. PROOFREADING REVIEW EXERCISE, ANSWER KEY

Compare the lefthand column below to the column on the right. Mark the righthand column so that, when corrections are made, it will match the lefthand column exactly.

WHICH CAME FIRST?	*all caps* Which Came First?
Were there no readers, there	Were ther no readers, there
certainly would be no writers;	certainly would not be writers; *no*
clearly therefore, the existence	clearling therefore, the existence
of writers depends upon the	of writers dependent upon the
existence of readers and, of	existents of readers and,
course, since the cause must	course, yet, because the case must *since*
be antecedent to the effect,	be antecedent to the cause, *effect*
readers existed before writers.	all readers existed before writers.
Yet, on the other hand, if there	Yet, on the other hand, If there
were no writers there could be	was no writer there could be *were*
no readers, so it would appear	no readers, so it appears *would*
that writers must be antecedent	that writers must be anticedent
to readers.	to readers.
--Horace Smith, quoted in The Love Affairs of a Bibliomaniac by Eugene Field	--Smith, quted in The Love Affair of a Bibliomaniac by Eugene Field *Horace*

94

PRACTICE 11. SPACING MARKS, ANSWER KEY

NEW VERSION ONLY

John Stuart Mill's inaugural address (as rector of the University
of St. Andrew) on February 1, 1867, included the following words:
"To question all things;--never to turn away from any difficulty,
to accept no doctrine either from ourselves or from other people
without a rigid scrutiny by negative criticism; letting no fallacy,
or incoherence, or confusion of thought, step by unperceived; above

all, to insist upon having the meaning of a word clearly understood
before using it, and the meaning of a proposition before assenting
to it;--these

are the lessons we learn from ancient dialecticians."

(margin annotations: align, less #, one line, move up, #, move down, #, ℃, less #)

PRACTICE 12. SPECIAL PROBLEMS, ANSWER KEY

Follow the instructions for each part of the following practice.

A. Mark the following word divisions for correction when they are wrong:

......~~Januar~~
~~y~~   Jan - u - ary

.......~~Febr~~
~~uary~~   Feb - ru - ary

........~~Mar~~
~~ch~~   March

..........~~A~~
~~pril~~   April

..........Ju-
ly

.........~~Aug~~
~~ust~~   Au - gust

......Septem-
ber

..........Oc-
tober

.........~~Nov~~
~~ember~~   No - vem - ber

........~~Dece~~
~~mber~~   De - cem - ber

B. Mark the righthand column so that, when it is corrected, it will match the lefthand column:

ADM William Jones, Senior was born in Roanoke, Va., on December 19, 1921. He received his Bachelor of Arts degree from Illinois College in 1942, the same year he joined the U.S. Navy as an ensign.	ADM ~~Admiral~~ Ⓦm. Jones, Ⓢr., was born in Roanoke, ~~Virginia~~, on ⒹDec. 19, 1921. He received his ⒷB.A. degree from ~~Ill.~~ ~~Coll.~~ in 1942, the same year he joined the ~~United States~~ Navy as an ~~ENS.~~

sp /. sp
Va.
sp
sp
College
Illinois
U.S.
ensign

96

C. Mark "round" to make "around." a⌢ ₍round

   Mark "long" to make "belong." be⌢ ₍long

   Mark "ward" to make "award." a⌢ ₍ward

   Mark "devil" to make "deviltry." devil₍ ⌢try

   Mark "van" to make "vanguard." van₍ ⌢guard

   Mark "in exact" to make "inexact." ɔ/ in⌢exact

   Mark "whole sale" to make "wholesale." ɔ/ whole⌢sale

   Mark "around" to make "a round." # a₍round

   Mark "belong" to make "be long." # be₍long

   Mark "award" to make "a ward." # a₍ward

   Mark "deviltry" to make "devil try." devil₍try #

   Mark "vanguard" to make "van guard." van₍guard #

   Mark "inexact" to make "in exact." in₍exact #

   Mark "wholesale" to make "whole sale." whole₍sale #

D. Mark the column at the right to match the column at the left.

surefire   sure⌿fire

rolltop   roll⌢er top

marketplace   market~in~e place

cardboard   card⌢o board

daydream   day⌢s dream

field day   field⌿y day   #

ground cover   ground⌿s cover   #

ice pick   ice⌿r pick   #

No one quality stands alone.   # /ɔ/# No⌢on⌢e quality stands alone.

Among you I see half with erring   Among you I see half⌿wit⌢h erring   #/ɔ/#
   ways.   ways.

Together we got her everything.   ɔ/ɔ/ɔ/# To⌢get⌢her we go⌢ther⌢every⌢thing.   #/ɔ/ɔ

97

PRACTICE 13. PROOFREADING REVIEW EXERCISE, ANSWER KEY

Part 1, Adding: Proofread the column on the right by comparing it to the column on the left. Mark it to add omitted characters, words, or passages.

ROMANCES

In ages when there were no books, when noblemen and princes themselves could not read, history or tradition was monopolized by the story-tellers. They inherited, generation after generation, the wondrous tales of their predecessors, which they retailed to the public with such additions of their own as they acquired information to supply them with. Anachronisms became of course very common, and errors of geography, of locality, of manners, equally so. Spurious genealogies were invented, in which Arthur and his knights, and Charlemagne and his paladins, were made to derive their descent from Aeneas, Hector, or some other of the Trojan heroes.

Part 2, Taking Out: Proofread the column on the right by comparing it to the column on the left. Mark it to take out any extra characters, words, or passages.

At a time when chivalry excited universal admiration, and when all the efforts of that chivalry were directed against the enemies of religion, it was natural that literature should receive the same impulse, and that history and fable should be ransacked to furnish examples of courage and piety that might excite increased emulation. Arthur and Charlemagne were the two heroes selected for this purpose.

Part 3, Replacing: Proofread the column on the right by comparing it to the column on the left. Mark for all replacements needed in characters, words, or passages, including changes of typeface or type style and transpositions. (Two ways of marking transpositions are correct. You may mark transpositions with the double loop and ⟨tr⟩, as on the answer keys, or you may simply mark transposed characters to be replaced with characters in the correct order.)

Arthur's pretensions were that he was a brave, though not always successful warrior; he had withstood with great resolution the arms of the infidels, that is to say, of the Saxons, and his memory was held in the highest estimation by his countrymen, the Britons, who carried with them into Wales, and into the kindred country of Armorica, or Brittany, the memory of his exploits, which their national vanity insensibly exaggerated, till the little prince of the Silures (South Wales) was magnified into the conqueror of England, of Gaul, and of the greater part of Europe. His genealogy was gradually carried up to an imaginary Brutus, and to the period of the Trojan War, and a sort of chronicle was composed in the Welsh, or Armorican, language which, under the pompous title of the History of the Kings of Britain, was translated into Latin by Geoffrey of Monmouth, about the year 1150. The Welsh critics consider the material of the work to have been an older history, written by St. Talian, Bishop of Asaph, in the seventh century.

Arthur's pretensions were that he was a brave, though not always successful warrior/ he had withheld with great warrior/ resolve the army of the infidels, that is to say, of the Saxons, and his memory was held in the highest estimation by his countrymen, the Britons, who carried into Wales with them, and into the kindred country of Armorica, or Brittany, the memories of his exploits, which their National vanity insensibly exaggerates, until the little prince of the Silures (South Wales) was magnified into the conqueror of England, of Gaul, and of the larger part of Europe. His geneology was gradually carried up to an imaginary Brutus, and to the period of the Trojan War, and a sort of service was composed in the Welsh, or American, language which, under the pompous title of The History Of the Kings of Britain, was translated into Latin by Jeffery of MonMouth, about the year 1150. The Welsh critics consider the material of the work to have been an elder history, written by Saint Talian, Bishop of Asaph, in the 7th century.

PRACTICE 13, ANSWER KEY (cont.)

Part 4, Adding, Taking Out, and Replacing: Proofread the column on the right by comparing it to the column on the left. Mark to add, to take out, and to replace anything necessary.

As to Charlemagne, though his real merits were sufficient to secure his immortality, it was impossible that his holy wars against the Saracens should not become a favorite topic for fiction. Accordingly, the fabulous history of these wars was written, probably towards the close of the eleventh century, by a monk, who, thinking it would add dignity to his work to embellish it with a contemporary name, boldly ascribed it to Turpin, who was Archbishop of Rheims about the year 773.

As to Charlemagne, Although his merits were sufficient to secure his immortality, it was not possible that his holy wars against the Saracens should not become a favoyite subject for fiction. Accordingly, the fabulous history of these wars was written, boldly ascribed to Turpin, who was Arch Bishop of Rheims about the year 773.

Part 5, Errors in Spacing and Positioning: Proofread the column on the right by comparing it to the column on the left. Mark for correction of all errors in spacing and for type to be moved where necessary.

These fabulous chronicles were for a while imprisoned in languages of local only or of professional access... The Anglo-Saxon was at that time used only by a conquered and enslaved nation... Norman French was spoken and understood by the nobility in the greater part of Europe, and therefore was a proper vehicle for the new mode of composition.

That language was fashionable in England before the Conquest, and became, after that event, the only language used at the court in London. As the various conquests of the Normans, and the enthusiastic valor of that extraordinary people, had familiarized the minds of men with the most marvellous events, their poets eagerly seized the fabulous legends of Arthur and Charlemagne, (and) translated them into the language of the day.

These fabulous chronicles were for a while imprisoned in languages of local only or of professional access... The Anglo-Saxon was at that time used only by a conquered and enslaved nation... Norman French alone was spoken and understood by the nobility in the greater part of Europe, and therefore was a proper vehicle for the new mode of composition. That language was fashionable in England before the Conquest, and became, after that event, the only language used at the court in London. As the various conquests of the Normans, and the enthusiastic valor of that extraordinary people, had familiarized the minds of men with the most marvellous events, their poets eagerly seized the fabulous legends of Arthur and Charlemagne, (and) translated them into the language of the day.

100

PRACTICE 13, ANSWER KEY (cont.)

Part 6, All Kinds of Errors: Proofread the column on the right by comparing it to the column on the left. Mark for all errors in type and spacing.

METRICAL ROMANCES

The earliest form in which romances appear is that of a rude kind of verse. In this form it is supposed they were sung or recited at the feasts of princes and knights in their baronial halls. The following specimen of the language and style of Robert de Beauvais, who flourished in 1257, is from Sir Walter Scott's Introduction to the Romance of Sir Tristram.

"Ne voil pas emmi dire,
Ici diverse la matyere..."

"I will not say too much about it,
So diverse is the matter..."

This is a specimen of the language which was in use among the nobility of England in the ages immediately after the Norman conquest. The following is a specimen of the English that existed at the same time among the common people. Robert de Brunne, speaking of his Latin and French authorities, says:--

"Als thai haf wryten and sayd
Haf I alle in myn Inglis layd,
In symple speeche as I couthe,
That is lightest in manne's mouthe.
Alle for the luf of symple men,
That strange Inglis cannot ken."

The "strange Inglis" being the language of the previous specimen.

101

PRACTICE 14. FINAL EXERCISE, ANSWER KEY

ING   PROVERBS FOR PROOFREAD~~ERS~~

(Comma) <u>Love is nearsighted.</u> When you are the writer, editor, typist, or typesetter proofreading your own work, you will almost surely suffer from myopia. You are too close to see all the errors. Get help.

<u>Familiarity breeds content.</u> When you see the same copy again and again through the different stages of production and revision, you may well miss new errors. Fresh eyes are needed.

y <u>If it's as plain as the nose on your face, everbody can see it but you.</u> Where is the reader most likely to notice errors? In a headline; in a title; in the first line, first paragraph, or first page of copy; and in the top lines of a new page. These are precisely the places where ed-

most itors and proofreaders are ~~very~~ likely to miss errors. Take extra care at every beginning.

[[<u>Mistakery loves company.</u> Errors often cluster. When you find one, look hard for

⊃ others near by.

(under- line) <u>When you change horses in midstream, you can get wet.</u> It's easy to overlook an error set in type that is different from the text face you are reading. Watch out when type changes to all caps, italics, boldface, small sizes, and large sizes. Watch

n out when underlines appear in typewritten copy.

<u>Glass houses invite stones.</u> Beware copy that discusses errors. When the subject is typographical quality, the copy must be typographically perfect. When the topic is errors in grammar or spelling, the copy must be error-free. Keep alert for words

ℓ like <u>typograhical</u> or <u>proofreading.</u> ~~Doub-~~
Dou- ~~le~~ check and triple check.
ble

The footbone conneckit to the kneebone?
Numerical and alphabetical sequences often
go awry. Check for omissions and duplications in page numbers, footnote numbers,
or notations in outlines and lists. Check
any enumeration, anything in alphabetical
order, and everything sequential (such as
as the path of arrows in a flowchart)

ꝃ/ footnote / page

ꝃ

ꝃ/ (period)

It takes two to boogie. An opening
parenthesis needs a closing parenthesis.
Brackets, quotation marks, and sometimes
dashes belong in pairs. Catch the
bachelors.

ꝃ

Every yoohoo deserves a yoohoo back. A
footnote reference mark or a first reference to a table of an illustraton is
termed a callout. Be sure a footnote begins on the same page as its callout. Be
sure a table or illustration follows its
callout as soon as possible.

r/ꝃ/i

Numbers can speak louder than words.
Misprints in numerals (figures) can be catastrophic. Take extraordinary care with
dollar figures and numbers in dates, statistics, tables, or technical text. Read
all numerals character by character; for
example, read "1979" as "one nine seven
nine." Be sure any figures in your hand
writing are unmistakable.

h

(hyphen)

Two plus two is twenty-two. The simplest math can go wrong. Do not trust
figures giving percentages and fractions
or the "total" lines in tables. Watch
for misplaced decimal points. Use your
calculator.

(align)

Above all, never assume that all is
well. As the saying goes, ass-u-me
makes an ass out of u an me.

o/d

Editorial Experts, Inc. (EEI), is a full-service publications firm located in Alexandria, VA. EEI's services include writing, editing, proofreading, word and data processing, design and graphics, abstracting, indexing, workshops for publications professionals, and temporary and permanent placement in the publications field. EEI plans and manages conferences and produces the publications arising from them. EEI also publishes the award-winning *Editorial Eye* newsletter and books in the editorial and publications field. Other books published by EEI include the following:

Substance and Style—Instruction and Practice in Copyediting
Provides an introduction to the basic skills of copyediting and serves as an excellent reference on grammar and editing.

Language On A Leash
A provocative collection of more than 40 essays on the English language to please word lovers everywhere.

The Expert Editor
A short course in editing compiled from the award-winning newsletter, *The Editorial Eye*, and aimed at the working editor and all people who work with words.

Stet! Tricks of the Trade for Writers and Editors
A collection of articles from *The Editorial Eye* newsletter.

Directory of Editorial Resources
Listings of the best courses, books, periodicals, and organizations for professional writers and editors. Published biennially.

Mark My Words: Instruction and Practice in Proofreading
Self-teaching book that includes text, exercises, and answer keys.

The Editorial Eye
Award-winning monthly newsletter for publications professionals. Please write for sample copy.

Editorial Experts, Inc.
66 Canal Center Plaza, Suite 200
Alexandria, VA 22314
703/683-0683

EXAMPLE OF SIMPLIFIED PROOFREADING MARKS

Proofreader's Marks

Corrected Copy

(caps)
(center)
EDUCATION (and) PRINTING
] UNDESIRABLE [

(move left) / ℓ
[Sir William Berkeley, who was (comma)
governor of Virginia, to 1652 from 1642
and again from 1660 to 1667;
summarized the attitudes of
most of the officials of his
ʃ day, ~~in his famous statement,~~
in his famous statement, "But, #
I thank God, there are no free

(less space) (
schools nor printing/ and I   (comma)
i hope we will not have these
hundred 100 years, for ~~education~~ has learning
brought ~~bruohgt~~ disobedience, and ~~he~~ her-esy
~~resy,~~ and sects into the world,
(align) and prin^t^i^n g has divulged them,
(less #) and ⁀ libels against the best
(lc) Government. God keep us from
(same line) both."
((Berkeley was in error; free (bad type)
schools had existed in Vir- ʃ part of underline
(move right) ginia, though printing had not.)
—August Klapper / (superscript 1)

EDUCATION AND PRINTING
UNDESIRABLE

Sir William Berkeley, who was
governor of Virginia from 1642
to 1652 and again from 1660 to
1667, summarized the attitudes
of most of the officials of his
day in his famous statement,
"But, I thank God, there are no
free schools nor printing, and
I hope we will not have these
hundred years, for learning has
brought disobedience, and her-
esy, and sects into the world,
and printing has divulged them,
and libels against the best
government. God keep us from
both." (Berkeley was in error:
free schools had existed in Virginia, though printing had not.)
—August Klapper[1]

(move down) /# ⌊1⌋In The Printer in Colonial
Williamsburg, 1969.
(underline)

1. In The Printer in Colonial
Williamsburg, 1969.